Legal Almanac Series No. 45

NEW LIFE STYLE

AND

THE CHANGING LAW

By

Libby F. Jessup, J.D.

1971

OCEANA PUBLICATIONS, INC.
Dobbs Ferry, New York

This is a newly revised edition of the forty-fifth number in a series of LEGAL ALMANACS which bring you the law on various subjects in nontechnical language. These books do not take the place of your attorney's advice, but they can introduce you to your legal rights and responsibilities.

(Former edition of Legal Almanac Number 45: Law for the Family Man, by Libby F. Jessup)

Manufactured in the United States of America

CONTENTS

INTRODUCTION

There is scarcely any aspect of life that is not touched by the law. The law is privy to most of our activities. Although everyone talks of "doing his own thing" the law is always to be reckoned with. Whether you are buying a house, or selling it; getting married, or divorced; sending your children to school, or keeping them home; going into business or getting out of it; buying or selling, for cash or on credit; borrowing or lending money; whether you are a college professor or carpenter; plumber or preacher; schoolteacher or storekeeper, the law is there.

There is, of course, nothing strange in this. We live in an organized society and the law consists of the rules by which society has chosen to be regulated. These rules are subject to constant revision and vary greatly with changes in attitudes, basic philosophy and economic conditions. In the early industrial days of this country, laws were passed to protect women in the labor market. Today, many of those same rules are being reexamined and challenged because, it is claimed, they have become the tools of discrimination and oppression.

Never before in the history of this country has there been greater soul-searching and more intense reexamination of the laws of our society. The changing philosophy of our times is reflected, although much too slowly in the opinion of many, in the changing law. New language has come into existence and technical terms are now on the tongue of even the most unlettered person, in new and personal context. Problems once thought to be the exclusive province of the government are now of general concern. Ecology, pollution, consumerism, the corporate state, equal rights for women and women's rights, population explosion, are a few of the concepts now the topics of daily discussion among all people, regardless of their station in life or their educational background.

v

In the last decade, our attitudes on marriage and divorce, inter-personal relations, population control, whether by birth control or abortion, have changed drastically. The "right" to conduct one's own business without governmental interference has been challenged when it endangers the public or conflicts with our concern for the environment or the physical or emotional well-being of persons employed in such business, and members of the general public for a multitude of other reasons.

Under our changing philosophy, greater emphasis is being placed on the rights and protection of children, the aged and other members of society under a disadvantage. Programs have been developed for the treatment, instead of punishment, of dope addicts, reflecting new thinking that dope addiction is a social or health problem, rather than a legal one. Information programs have been instituted at public expense. The very right to live, guaranteed by the Constitution of the United States, has been imbued with new meaning. Welfare clients recently took over private premises for their personal use and claimed it to be in furtherance of their right to live, a position which is legally untenable under present law but which may tomorrow be given serious attention. It has been said that it is among the duties of society to enforce the rights of humanity.

A new awareness has served to remind people of their own power and this power is slowly but surely being translated into legislative action. Many changes have been made in the law to protect the private individual against the corporate advertiser, the banks and other lending institutions and even his own government (e.g. Vietnam - war status); to protect him in his right to get from suppliers what he thinks he is getting; to be informed (truth-in-lending, for example); to protect his safety (automobile legislation, for example); and other consumer legislation designed for his welfare.

The changes made are numerous and those which will be made are probably legion. This manual will serve to highlight basic rules and regulations controlling our actions at this time and to cast some light on the road ahead.

Libby F. Jessup

April, 1971

PART I.

LIFE STYLE OF THE FAMILY

In no other areas are the changes in thinking attutides more evident than in personal relations. They touch the very lives of every person intimately. Marriages are more easily made; divorces have been liberalized. Children's rights vis-a-vis their parents and others are strengthened so that society will step in when necessary to protect a child, even against his parents. Society, on the whole, is interfering less and less in the relationship between a man and a woman but more and more to protect the old, young, handicapped or other persons, disadvantaged, either by physical or economic conditions, or by the prejudices of their fellow man. Women's status improves, slowly to be sure, but continuously. Birth control and abortion laws have received official approval and abortions are now not considered as something short of criminal, as, in most cases, they used to be. At least 38 states now permit abortion. The threat of population explosion has caused the release of information relevant to birth control; methods calculated to prevent conception, and to permit abortions. The attitude towards birth control and abortions has so changed that it is safe to predict that these matters will soon be left to the woman to resolve, possibly with the assistance of her physician.

Marrying has become easier in several states by reducing the age of consent; some states have dispensed with the waiting period after issuance of marriage license. Also, laws prohibit - ing mixed marriages (iniscegenation) have been declared uncon - stitutional.

The whole institution of marriage is under serious scrutiny and attack. There have been serious proposals that marriages should be based on a three year contract between the parties, renewable by them at the expiration of the period. However, in spite of changing attitudes and the few changes mentioned above, the formal requirements of marriage remain virtually unchanged.

Divorce laws in general have been relaxed so that it is

easier for partners to an unsatisfactory marriage to call it quits. The tendency today is to get away from the theory that the failure of the marriage, and its legal termination, must be based on fault. California now has only two grounds for divorce -- irreconcilable differences and incurable insanity. New Jersey and Wisconsin similarly have "no-fault" divorce. New York, which used to recognize only one ground for divorce (adultery) has added several.

Chapter 1

MARRIAGE -- RIGHTS AND DUTIES AS SPOUSE AND PARENT

Marriage has been looked upon as a contract between a man and a woman, suffering from no legal impediments, and the state as a silent partner. Certain well-defined consequences flow from the status developing from this contract. It cannot be cancelled or vitiated solely by the parties, but only by compliance with the legal requirements of the state in which severance is sought. Duties are created not only in the parties to the marriage, but in the state, in the issue of the marriage and in the marriage itself.

A marriage cannot exist but by grace of the state. Even the so-called common law marriage, contracted without formal license, must comply with the requirements defined by law. In the absence of the existence of conditions defined by law, a common law marriage is not valid.

The validity of a marriage is tested by the laws of the state where it is made. Each state, being sovereign over its citizens, sets down its own requirements for a valid marriage to exist. The requirements for the various states are set down in Chart I. Basically, the requirements can be grouped into several categories.

Persons Who May Marry

As stated above, a man and woman not under legal impediment may marry, upon compliance with the technical requirements set forth. Persons related within prohibited degrees of consanguinity or kinship may not marry and such a marriage is said to be void. A marriage between persons one or both of whom are legally married to another is also said to be void. To say that a marriage is void is to say that there is no legal marriage between the parties, with all of the consequences of non-legal status.

3

Any other marriage, properly contracted, is valid. However, there are certain circumstances under which certain valid marriages may be terminated at the instance of one of the parties. These are said to be voidable marriages. Voidable marriages are valid until affirmative action is taken by the party having the right to do so to terminate the marriage.

A marriage is voidable if one of the parties is underage, or is a person incapable of consent; if a fraud was practiced by one party on the other; and for other reasons specified in the laws of the various states. A voidable marriage can be terminated by action on the part of the party against whom the fraud was perpetuated or who suffers from the disability indicated above. Such a marriage is usually ended by annulment of the marriage. An annulment usually sets the marriage aside from its inception on the theory that the marriage would not have been contracted but for the fraud or the disability of one of the parties.

Technical Requirements for Marriage

A marriage license is the basic requirement for a valid marriage. However, generally a marriage license will be issued only after the parties have obtained a physician's certificate that they are free from venereal disease, based on an examination made within a specified period (30 days, in New York). There may be a waiting period before the license is issued. There generally is a waiting period after the issuance of the marriage license and before the solemnization of the marriage. A marriage license is usually valid for a limited period of days. In some cases, a judge will waive (or dispense with) the waiting period. During the way years, when young men were about to be shipped overseas, a judge would often waive the waiting period.

A marriage may be solemnized either by civil or religious ceremony. It does not matter, as long as the parties state in the presence of two witnesses that they take each other as husband and wife. A marriage solemnized in accordance with the requirements of a particular religion is valid.

Some jurisdictions permit proxy marriages where a stand-in takes the vows in the place of and on behalf of the missing spouse. Such marriages are invalid in most states. But, if the proxy marriage is legal in the state where contracted it must be recognized by other jurisdictions.

A minor (in most jurisdications, males under 21 and females under 18) may not marry without the consent of the parents. A marriage of persons marrying without parental consent does not invalidate the marriage but renders the clerk liable to a fine.

Common Law Marriages

A common law marriage is one contracted between the parties without compliance with the technical requirements of a ceremonial marriage. Before a common law marriage will be found to exist there must be clear and convincing evidence of its existence, the parties must have the capacity to marry, that is, be free of any of the encumbrances which would invalidate any marriage, and be of the age of consent at the time the marriage was contracted. The marriage must have been intended at the time the parties entered into the relationship; there must be open cohabitation as husband and wife. The parties must hold themselves out as husband and wife in the community in which they live.

Common law marriages are now illegal in most states. However, common law marriages, contracted at such time and in such place as they were legal, continue to be so although the law has changed as far as any new common law marriages are concerned.

Rights and Duties Springing from Marriage

Name. Many rights arise out of the marriage relationship. For example, a woman has the right to use her husband's name. This does not mean that she must use her husband's name. Many women continue to use their maiden names for business and professional reasons. But her right to use his name survives even a divorce. However, if a marriage is annulled, a wife may be barred from using her husband's name based on the reasoning that there was no valid marriage from the start. If a divorce is obtained for the wife's adultery, the husband may prohibit the wife from using his name.

Support. A husband has the duty to support his wife and is not excused from such duty even though he is a minor, or incapacitated or incompetent, as long as he is financially able to do so. A husband may not destroy this obligation by giving up a job or by giving priorty to subordinate obligations. A wife may be reimbursed for expenses although she has sufficient funds herself to take care of them. In some cases, however, a wife may be required to support her husband if he is about to become a public charge.

While a wife's misconduct may relieve a husband from his duty to support her, it does not relieve him of the duty to support the children of the marriage. This duty of the husband to support a wife may not be contracted away by the parties even though the wife has money to take care of herself. The duty of a husband to support a wife continues after divorce if the wife obtained the divorce. An agreement between the parties as to support and other financial affairs will be respected by the courts unless it is patently inadequate or inequitable to the wife. In such case, the courts will do justice as the circumstances warrant. Also, the courts will respect a lump sum agreement negotiated by the parties, even though the terms differ from those contained in a divorce decree granted by the court. Alimony payments cease when the husband dies, unless the parties specifically agree that they shall survive his death.

Effects of remarriage upon support provisions. Generally, a court will relieve a divorced husband of the duty of support to his ex-wife if she remarries because the feeling is that the new husband should support his wife.

A husband is under no limitation as to the transfer of his property, unless he has represented to his wife that he has such property and his actions constitute a fraud upon his wife. Where, under a separation agreement, a husband owes his wife money, she is his creditor and a transfer of his assets would be as much of a fraud as if they were not married. Such a transfer could be set aside. This may even be true in cases where the husband is not in default and is up to date on his payments. The rights of children to be supported are similarly treated so that they may become their father's creditors based on support payments which he owes them.

Husband and Wife

"You've come a long way, baby" has an element of truth in it when applied to a wife. Until the 19th century and for many

years after that, a married woman was considered something between a chattel (or possession) and a not very bright child. Marriage did not free a woman but made her husband her master and
caretaker. A married woman could not hold property or dispose
of it in her own right. She could not enter a binding contract.
Today, much of this has changed. Married Women's Acts define
the separate property of married women, and recognize the right
of women to enter into binding contracts. They release a married woman's property from her husband's control. By and large,
married women today are free to make all types of contracts and
to acquire, sell, mortgage, control and dispose of real and personal property without any action or acquiescence on the part of
their husbands.

A number of states (among them, California and Texas)
have what is known as community property. Community property
laws provide that all property acquired during the marriage (with
some exceptions) and not specifically the property of either spouse,
belongs to both of them. On death the surviving spouse gets one-
half. The balance is disposed of in accordance with the laws of
the state of domicile or as the will of the deceased spouse indicates.

While these laws are granting greater rights to women,
vestiges of the old philosophy can be seen in the laws of descent
and distribution. In many states, for example, a husband generally gets a life estate to all of his wife's real property while a
wife will get only one third interest in such property.

In most jurisdictions, the husband decides where the family will live and determines the domicile (which is the legal residence) for his wife as well.

In the absence of an agreement, a wife who works for her
husband is not entitled to a salary but the presumption is the other
way if the husband works for his wife in her business. In other
words, he is entitled to a salary. Under the old common law,
the husband of a woman who worked for a stranger was entitled to
her salary. This is, of course, no longer true.

Today a woman may sue anyone, including her husband,
for injury to her person, property or character. She is also solely
liable for any wrong she may commit, unless such acts were at
the instigation of her husband or under his coercion, in which
cases, he would be joined as a party. A married woman is responsible for her criminal acts even though they were performed
at the instigation or under the duress of her husband.

7

While the primary duty to support children is that of the father, a mother may also be chargeable for their support if the father cannot be found or is dead or is incapable of supporting them. Support for a child includes many things -- necessary shelter, food, clothing, medical and hospital care, education and other reasonable and proper items. The quality of the care and the extent of the education vary with the economic conditions of the parent. In general, the standards the parent sets for himself serve as guidelines for the support to which his children are entitled. This brings up interesting questions. In today's climate, where many children are breaking with their parents over basic philosophy and in many other respects, just what duties does a parent owe a recalcitrant offspring? To what extent can the parent impose his will on the child or condition his support upon compliance with disciplines the father considers proper?

These are not easy questions to answer. The answer will depend on many factors -- such as the age of the child, the nature of the recalcitrance, the nature of the conditions imposed by the parent. Thus, a young child who refuses to follow dietary restrictions imposed by a parent or refuses to study could probably not be turned out into the streets and must be supported. But a college student who refuses to study and cuts classes, may well be required to earn his own spending money. However, if a student wants to go to college away from home, and the family can afford it, and the facts are such as to persuade a court that the child might find attendance at a college out of town conducive to his development, it would probably decide that the parent would be responsible for the child's education and would be under a duty to pay the child's tuition. However, this matter is under litigation at the present time. It appears that a parent cannot be autocratic with a child as long as the child is engaged in reasonable conduct.

A child may release a parent from the duty to support him by his acts. A son who moves out of the parental home, gets himself a job, or sets up his own apartment, or a daughter who gets married are said to be emancipated. That is to say, they become independent of their parents and are no longer subject to their control. They have, by their own acts, cut the ties that bound them to their parents. As the child is released from parental control, so are the parents freed from their duties as parents.

8

Where duties are found to exist, however, they are so strongly entrenched in the law, that criminal sanctions may be imposed to insure their observance. In New York, for example, a parent who abandons a child under 14 years of age is guilty of a felony; a parent failing to support a child under 16 is guilty of a misdemeanor.

When a person supplies a minor with services or items considered by law as "necessaries", he may hold the parent responsible for payment for the services or items.

Stepparents have the same relative duties towards a stepchild as a natural parent has towards his own children. The parents of illegitimate children have similar duties.

Most states have adopted the Uniform Support of Dependents Law, the terms of which describe the duties of a husband towards his wife, a father's duties towards children under 21, a mother's duties for the support of the children under 21, where the father is dead, disabled or incapacitated; a wife's duty to support a husband who is incapable of supporting himself and about to become a public charge.

Child's Name

A child has the right to use the father's name but there are circumstances under which a child may be permitted to use another name. If the mother remarries, for example, the children might well want to take the name of the stepfather for the sake of convenience or to save themselves embarrassment. The children's welfare is the controlling factor.

Any person may change his name at will, without any court action, unless fraud and deceit is the motivation for the change. Generally, however, a change of name is effected by a court order, in order to fix the time of the change and to keep the records straight.

Privileges Conferred by the Marital Status

Neither a husband nor a wife may be compelled to testify as to any confidential matters between them, unless the other spouse agrees. A communication made by one spouse to the other is presumed to be confidential. This privilege even survives death

9

and divorce. The privilege may be asserted by the person against whom it is sought to use the testimony. The privilege may be waived by the person having the right to assert it or by his failure to assert the privilege. However, if one spouse commits a wrong against the other, the privilege is lost on the theory that the words may constitute part of the tort. Also, a husband or a wife may testify in actions where either is a party and in actions between them.

Domicile or Residence

It has been said that a husband sets the marital domicile. But this right is no longer absolute. It must be exercised with due regard for the health, welfare and peace of mind of the wife. A wife may, on the other hand, choose her domicile if she is entitled to a divorce or if the parties have agreed to separate, and are living apart by agreement. Domicile has been defined as the legal residence. A person may have several residences but only one legal domicile.

The domicile of a minor is set by the parent's domicile. It no longer belongs exclusively to the father. Emancipated children have the right to select their own domicile. A widow may change the domicile of her children. Once a domicile is estabfished, the burden of proof to change it is on the person claiming the change.

Adoption

Adoption is the legal procedure whereby one becomes the legal parent of a child or person not born to him or her. An adoptive parent acquires all the rights and duties of a parent toward such person. The natural parent in such a case loses all rights in and duties toward such child.

In general, an adult unmarried person, adult husband and wife together, a married couple, not necessarily adult, vis-a-vis a child born to either of them out of wedlock, may adopt children.

Adoption may be on a private placement basis or from authorized agencies. The consent to adoption may be required of a foster child over a certain age; of a mother of a child born out of wedlock; of the parents of a child born in wedlock; of any person

10

having custody of the child. Generally, if a parent has abandoned a child, consent is not required. A child surrendered for adoption may sometimes suffer, as recent litigation in New York proves, when the mother who gave birth to the illegitimate child has a change of heart and wishes to withdraw her consent.

The consent of the natural parents is not required if a parent is deprived of his civil rights, or has been divorced for adultery, or is incompetent, mentally defective, or a habitual drunkard. Where custody of a child has been removed from the natural parent for cruelty or neglect, consent is not required. Where the adopted person is 18 or over, the courts may dispense with parental consent to the adoption.

An adopted child is in most respects treated the same as a natural child for the purpose of inheritance. It used to be said that an adopted child could inherit <u>from</u> his adoptive parents but not <u>through</u> them. In other words, if his father's sister died and left property to the adoptive parent who had already died by that time, the adoptive child could not take it because he was taking through the adoptive parent and not from him directly.

Although it is extremely unusual, adoptions may be abrogated or terminated. It may be done by consent, by or on behalf of the child because he is being maltreated by his foster parents, or by the foster parent if the child is intractable and incorrigible.

Illegitimate Children

As indicated above, illegitimate children today enjoy most of the rights of natural children born in wedlock. The question of legitimacy of a child has been raised in an interesting context. Artificial insemination, or the impregnation of a woman with the sperm of an unidentified man, where the marriage had produced no children, is a practice which permits a married couple to have children when they would otherwise be childless. In some instances, a child born as a result of artificial insemination has been branded as illegitimate. This view has not been supported in the courts although it has been much discussed.

11

Chapter 2

BREAKUP OF THE MARRIAGE

Whatever the reasons, the fact is that more and more marriages fail. The growing consensus of opinion appears to be that when a husband and wife decide they are incompatible, they should be able to dissolve the marriage without any attempt at allocating fault and without punishment or penalty for their failure. While the grounds for divorce or termination of the marriage have been liberalized, the traditional grounds have for the most part and in most states been preserved. It is likely that in the years to come, the traditional grounds based upon fault will either be eliminated or will fall into disuse and the basis for divorce or termination of the marriage will be simply incompatability.

At the present time, there are several ways in which a marital relationship may legally end. These are annulment, divorce and dissolution (this last ground is available in some states, only). Termination of marriage by these means is complete, in that the marriage itself is a thing of the past (although this does not mean that obligations arising out of the marital status do not continue) and the parties are free, in most instances, to remarry. Remarriage may be conditioned on restrictions imposed by the laws of the state, or by the judge granting the divorce decree.

Marriage rights may also be destroyed by a legal separation, either judicial (that is, granted by a court decree) or by agreement between the parties. Parties who are merely separated may not remarry unless they obtain a decree of divorce, annulment or dissolution of the marriage.

Annulment

Annulment proceeds on the theory that the marriage was invalid when entered into because of the existence of certain conditions. Among the reasons for annulling a marriage are the following: the non-age of the party seeking the annulment; the insanity

12

of the spouse; impotence of the husband; fraud or duress exerted upon the party seeking the annulment. In the case of fraud, the fraud must be as to material fact and the party defrauded must seek remedy promptly after he discovers it and must not resume the marital relationship after the discovery of the fraud; if he does, he is said to have condoned (or forgiven) the fraud. Misrepresentation as to the following has been found to be fraud as to a material fact: concealment of a previous marriage; concealment of a disease; misrepresentation as to chastity or previous pregnancy; refusal to have children; promise to have religious ceremony without any such intention.

Divorce

Divorce is a termination of the marriage, generally for causes which arose during the marriage. Every state has its own grounds for divorce. Whether a person seeks a divorce or an annulment or a dissolution, there are certain formal requirements which must be complied with and certain conditions which must exist before the courts of that state will act on his request.

It is said that the courts must have jurisdiction of the matter (i.e., the marriage); the persons (domicile). Bona fide residence or domicile is probably the single most important formal requirement. Residence requirements range from 6 weeks in Nevada to five years in Massachusetts, for non-residents who have not lived in the state as husband and wife. Grounds for divorce range from adultery to violent temper tantrums, indignities or incompatability. Most states allow divorce for spouse's conviction for a felony, drunkenness, non-support or if he is condemned to life imprisonment. Many states allow divorce, today, if the parties have been separated for a specified period of time. Certain facts in some states will be the basis for an annulment or dissolution but not for a divorce. Continued absence of a spouse with reason to believe him dead may permit the courts to grant an annulment. The legal effect is the same in that the marriage is legally terminated.

What makes a divorce legally binding on both spouses? This is not a simple question. The only way for a person to get a valid divorce is to get it in the state where the parties were married or lived together or had domicile. It may be that the grounds permitted in that state are not adequate to permit divorce in a specific case. In that event, the parties might move to a more lenient state which does permit divorce on other grounds, establish a bona fide residence (which means establishing evidence of intention to live there permanently) and living there for the period of time required by the laws of that state. If the spouse answers the complaint, there is generally found to be jurisdiction.

There is no question that a divorce in the home state is generally desirable. If procedural requirements are complied with, it can rarely be challenged by the divorced spouse. A divorce obtained in another state is generally valid if the divorced spouse appears in the action. The greatest doubt as to the validity of a divorce exists as to the so-called "ex parte" divorce. An ex parte divorce is one where the defendant did not appear and therefore did not submit to the jurisdiction of the court and is not barred from raising objections. In these cases, unless the plaintiff was really a resident of the state, the divorce may be upset.

Judicial Separation

This is a separation brought about by court decree. In effect, the court finds that a party is justified in living apart from his spouse. The parties are still legally married and therefore are not free to remarry. The decree generally provides for custody of the children and support and maintenance for the wife and children, as well as a division of the property. Many grounds exist for the granting of a decree of separation -- cruelty, non-support, insanity, drunkenness, adultery. A legal separation will be nullified if the parties cohabit or if they ask the court to nullify the separation.

Valid separation agreements between the parties achieve the same results as a court decree of separation, except that disobedience of the court decree renders the person subject to contempt of court.

Alimony

In any of the actions mentioned above, a woman is entitled to alimony even before the issues have been resolved between the parties. Alimony granted while the trial is pending is called

14

temporary alimony. After the trial, the court may fix permanent alimony and support for any children of the marriage. The court may fix counsel fees. The matter of alimony and counsel fees is in the discretion of the court which takes into consideration the financial condition of the woman, her husband, the services to be rendered by the attorneys, the needs of the children and the woman, and other pertinent facts. There is one school of thought that alimony is a holdover from the days when a husband controlled and owned all the marital property and a wife was entirely dependent upon him for all necessities (alimony and counsel fees have been so classified). Today, with so much property in the hands of women, it may be argued that alimony is an anachronism of days gone by.

Permanent alimony is awarded a woman when she succeeds in her action. She must be free of guilt. Some states take a different view on this, and leave the matter of alimony to the discretion of the court after consideration of the facts -- such as the length of the marriage, ability of husband to pay, needs and resources of the wife. A husband may be required to put up security for the payments. Alimony awards may be modified to meet the changing circumstances of the parties.

Remarriage of Divorced Parties

The laws of the states vary greatly as to remarriage. In a few states, the guilty party may not remarry, or may not remarry the corespondent, or may not remarry for a number of years, or only with the court's consent. This limitation is also in the process of reexamination and it may soon be that all states will abolish limitations on remarriage.

Chapter 3

WOMEN'S RIGHTS

In the course of the discussion of family and personal rights above, we have mentioned changes effected in the status of women. In spite of the many changes made, many inequitites still exist. Agitation for equality comes not just from women's groups but from government sources and disinterested sources as well.

Many states have enacted laws which prevent or make illegal discrimination against women in employment (for example, not allowing women to work at night or overtime; not permitting women to work after a pregnancy). But many states still permit discriminatory practices by not prohibiting them.

Much remains to be done in this field and it is part of the changing scene that society is acutely aware of the problem. In today's climate, it is safe to say that we may expect tremendous changes in this area within the next several decades.

Before the enactment of the Civil Rights Act of 1964, only two states prohibited discrimination against women in employment. Now, it is prohibited by the laws of at least 27 states. In 1969, the Equal Employment Opportunity Commission found that laws originally intended to protect women from exploitation in labor or from working in certain types of jobs, failed to take into consideration the capabilities, preferences and capacities of individual women and tended more to discriminate against than to protect women. The Commission concluded that such laws and regulations would no longer be considered a defense to an otherwise estab - lished unlawful employment practice charge.

35 states now have laws requiring equal pay for women for equal owrk. Many states have relaxed the old rule prohibiting women from working extra hours, or during off-hours.

Commissions on the status of women have been established in practically all states. Many significant changes have resulted from the activities of these commissions. The general attitude now is that women should be granted equal status with men, even though at times it would mean that women would lose protective legislation. But, as indicated above, the feeling now is that the protection was either non-existent or was used as a subterfuge for the exploitation of women, or the protection was bought at the price of discrimination. Considering the greater independence of women today, both socially and economically, it may well be that protective legislation is now archaic.

Chapter 4

CHILDREN IN SOCIETY

In the past, in our zeal to protect children, even against their own acts, we have sometimes deprived them of rights no one would dream of withholding from an adult. Thus, in juvenile courts, we have denied them the right to counsel. Often, our best intentioned acts work an injustice. In a recent case, the United States Supreme Court handed down a decision which extended to juveniles accused of delinquency, certain constitutional rights which previously had been reserved for adults accused of crimes. Among these rights are the right against self-incrimination, timely notice of the charges against them and the right to counsel, the right to confront witnesses.

The fact that such a decision was necessary is some proof of the failure of the juvenile courts to achieve the goals which had been set for them when they were organized. The fact is that juvenile crime has risen, that there is a great deal of recidivism, or return to crime or delinquency, that the delinquency charge is a stigma which perhaps compels a return to illegal acts, and that institutionalizing of the person charged with juvenile delinquency even for treatment is a deprivation of personal liberty.

There are those who will claim that the decision referred to above is a step backward in the treatment of delinquents because the burden of defending them shifts to an attorney whose main purpose is to seek the release of the minor. It is a serious question whether in the long run the attorney who is interested in getting a dismissal of charges for his client and whose expertise is measured by the success he has in securing leniency for his client, is not in fact doing his client a disservice, perhaps barring him from much needed therapeutic treatment. Of course, a competent and socially oriented attorney, interested in the rehabilitation of an errant minor, might very well suggest that treatment and not freedom is the best thing for his client. He might thereby achieve two desirable ends: preserve the constitutional rights of his client and assist in his rehabilitation.

To cope with the mounting drug addiction problem, more realistic approaches have been adopted. Penalties for the use of marijuana have been reduced; stricter controls have been imposed on the use and the sale of hallucenogens and the hard drugs. In line with this, the U.S. Department of Justice has been ordered to develop a Model State Narcotics and Drug Act, for consideration and adoption by the states. Uniformity in a law of this nature is desirable, not only from an enforcement point of view, but because it will be prepared only after an intense study of the problem of addiction, and will be more effective in combatting the basic problem of addiction.

Studies have been made to determine whether genetic factors might account for criminality or juvenile delinquency. If it is discovered that this is so, it might be possible to control criminality when it is first manifested in young behavior.

Efforts have been made to increase the employment opportunities for teenagers on the theory that a busy young person will be less apt to get into trouble and that life will have more significance to him if he is participating in society. Also, economically speaking, a poor person who gets a job might be less apt to do illegal acts.

The fate of illegitimate children has been improved. The states have enlarged the group of persons eligible to become adoptive parents, by removing some of the traditional restrictions, so that more children born out of wedlock will be able to have the warmth of a family rather than indifferent institutional care.

Child abuse has been receiving much attention. The parent who feels his child is his property, may subject the child to unusual hardships or inhuman treatment. Many states have passed child abuse laws, or are more strictly enforcing them, to the extent that a child may be removed from the custody of a parent who is abusive towards him. Thus the rights of parents which have been described as "sacred, natural and inalienable" may, in the interest of the children, be abrogated.

PART II

ECONOMICS AND THE NEW LIFE STYLE

Chapter 5

EARNING A LIVING AND PROTECTION OF THE RIGHT

To a great extent, the limits of fair play between an employer and his employees have been defined, both by statutory law and by judicial decision. These rights fall into three general categories: 1) Those which guarantee to the worker the ability and right to deal with his employer on an equal basis (i.e., Collective Bargaining); 2) those which protect and insure his capacity to work i.e., those which compensate him for injuries received in the course of his employment (Workmen's Compensation), and those which compensate him for illness or inability to work (Disability Insurance) or because work is unavailable (Unemployment Insurance), or because he is overage and too old to work (Social Security) ; and 3) those rights which require equal opportunity in employment (i.e., not to be discriminated against, for reasons of race, color, creed, sex or age).

More specifically, a worker has the following undisputed rights:

He has the right to join a labor union and to bargain collectively with his employer. The law has long recognized the economic and sociological need for combinations of workers to balance the corporate powers of the employer.

A worker has the right not to be discriminated against. Most states have established commissions to deal with the problems of discrimination in employment and other areas. A federal judge has recently ruled that failure to hire a qualified person because he has filed complaints of violations of Equal Employment Opportunity Laws against a prior employer was itself a violation of the Federal Civil Rights Act of 1964.

Minimum Wages and Maximum Hours of Employment

The federal government and the various states all have passed laws regulating the hours of employment and setting minimum wages within their jurisdictions. In some instances, the law

23

applies only to women and children, or is restricted in application to certain industries. The tendency is, however, to apply the laws generally. At the present time, the federal minimum wage is $1.60 per hour. A few states provide for a minimum wage greater than that set by the federal government. Minimum wages and maximum hours are set forth in Chart 2.

Minimum wages and limitations of the hours of employment were originally effective as to women and children only because they were the groups most often exploited and discriminated against. We may, in the future, see a change in this because these laws, designed to protect women and children, have actually been used as tools of discrimination. In many states, the provisions of the laws limiting the hours of employment for women have been repealed.

Child Labor Laws

Child labor is controlled and restricted in most jurisdictions, not only as to hours of employment, but also as to type of employment, whether school is in session, the ages of the children. In addition, there are technical requirements, such as "working papers" and certificates of employment for children of school age.

Employment Benefits

Today a man's working ability is regarded as probably the most important investment he has to make. This investment is protected in several ways and under different circumstances.

a. <u>Workmen's Compensation</u>. All states have Workmen's Compensation laws, which provide for payments to be made to the employee in the event of injury suffered by him in the course of his employment, or to his heirs if he should die as a result of such injuries. The funds for such payments are provided for by insurance, either under private insurance plans or state plans. The total cost of Workmen's Compensation is paid for by the employer. A few categories of employers are exempt from provisions of Workmen's Compensation. Sometimes coverage is required only in hazardous industries, sometimes charitable organizations and governmental employers are not covered. Casual

24

workers are generally not covered. Workmen's Compensation also covers diseases resulting from employment as well as physical injuries from accidents.

b. <u>Disability Insurance</u>. Disability insurance compensates an employee who cannot work because of a disability resulting not from his employment but from some outside cause, or by reason of his general state of health.

c. <u>Unemployment Insurance</u>. This program is part of the Federal Social Security Program, but it is administered by the state in which the employee works. It provides for the payment of benefits to those who are unemployed, through no fault of their own, although ready, willing and able to do so, i.e., when there is no employment available to them. A person may not collect benefits under this program if his unemployment is due to his own conduct, or if he quits a job without good cause, or if he refuses to accept suitable employment. Benefits are paid for a specific period of time and at a stated rate, only as long as the worker continues to be unemployed within this period. There is usually a waiting period before benefits become payable. After a person becomes entitled to benefits, they are payable weekly, usually at a statutory minimum. Some states provide for allowances to deoendents of unemployed workers.

The Federal Unemployment Tax Act upon which the above insurance is based, itself deals only with the tax aspects. It declares who is liable for the tax, what compensation is taxable and the rate of the tax. It also sets the conditions for crediting a state with payment of unemployment taxes. In 1935, the Federal Unemployment Act was passed to encourage states to enact their own unemployment insurance acts. To do this, the Congress passed an act (described above) which imposed a 3% tax on employers. The federal law made no provision for the payment of benefits to unemployed persons. Instead, it provided for credits (up to 90% of the 3% tax paid) to a state for payments made by the state under its own unemployment act. All states have now passed unemployment insurance acts. The federal government polices the state laws and their administration by its ability to withhold payments if a state's laws do not meet the standards set by the federal government.

All employer contributions made under this program are paid into the United States Treasury. The federal government finances the supervision of the state unemployment insurance programs out of the funds remaining in its hands after paying the credits due the states.

    d. <u>Social Security</u>. Social Security is insurance against the day when the worker is retired from the labor market. Everyone is familiar with the Social Security program, which had its genesis in the depression. The basic program guarantees to a worker subsistence during his years of retirement, very much as pensions do. The employer and employee both make contributions, in equal amount, based upon the amount of the earnings up to a specified maximum amount of earnings (at present, this maximum is $7800; due to rise to a base of $9000 in 1972).

    All sums collected through Social Security are paid into the United States Treasury as Internal Revenue collections and appropriated to the Federal Old Age Survivors Insurance Trust Fund. The purpose of these funds are three fold, -- payment of what the law describes as "Old-age and Survivors Insurance Benefits", Disability Insurance Benefits and Hospital Insurance Benefits for the Aged.

    Retirement and Disability benefits at the present time range from $64 a month, based on earnings of $76 or less per month, to $250.70 per month, based on earnings of $649-$650 per month. The rates of payment are at the present time in the process of being increased. These payments constitute the primary insurance and are payable to the retired worker himself. They also form the basis for payments to the family and survivors of a deceased employee. Disability payments are made to a worker who is under 65 (if a man) or 62 (if a woman), who is disabled and has 20 quarters of covered employment over the last 40 quarters and has filed for benefits. The amount of disability payments are the same as if the covered worker had reached retirement age. There is a six-month waiting period before benefits become payable. A person who is getting Workmen's Compensation as well as disability may have the disability payments reduced.

    While Social Security resembles insurance and pensions, it differs in that if the worker dies and leaves no dependents, no payments, except for funeral expenses, are made to his heirs. Furthermore, if he does not stop working at age 65, or if he earns more than a set amount he is not entitled to benefits until he reaches the age of 72, at which time he may receive both benefits and earnings. Nor does the worker build up a fund against which he may draw if he is pressed for money. In other words, there is no cash surrender value in social security insurance. Thus, it is obvious that social security is only partial coverage and cannot be used before retirement, death or disability occurs.

The rights described above are now well-established. Important gains have been made in many areas affecting the wage earner. In 1968, a federal law was passed which would exempt from garnishment about 75% of the wage earner's disposable salary or 30 times the existing minimum wage, whichever is greater. An employer is prohibited from firing an employee whose salary has been garnished for one indebtedness.

There is also a Uniform Consumer Credit Code which would exempt from garnishment 75% of disposable earnings or 40 times existing federal minimum wages, whichever is greater. (New York permits 10% of gross income.) It prohibits any employer from discharging an employee regardless of the number of garnishments against his salary. It would furthermore prohibit any garnishment of salary before a judgment had been obtained against the worker by the creditor. While this code has not been generally adopted, many states have laws which protect the wages of a working man from unreasonable garnishment or discharge from employment because of garnishment. Some creditors tried to get around the law, by having the debtor execute an assignment of wages for the amount of the debt, but the United States Department of Labor recently ruled that such an assignment is legally unenforcible. In New York, Michigan, Hawaii and Montana, an employee is protected from being discharged because of garnishment. Other states prohibit discharge of an employee unless the number of garnishments exceed a stated number. (See Morganstern, Legal Almanac Series #66, Oceana, 1971.)

Minimum wages have generally increased and broader application of minimum wage laws is getting to be the rule, although many exceptions still exist. Most states permit the payment of lower wages to young employees or apprentices who are not experienced.

Over 40 states require the payment of prevailing wages to persons employed on public works. While, in general, labor legislation does not apply to agricultural workers, at the present time, there is a movement to extend to this group the benefits enjoyed by most other employees.

27

In spite of all that has been done to improve the status of the worker, there is still much that can be done to give him greater security and also to protect him against occurrences not previously included -- such as inflation and fraud. There has also been very serious discussion of the possibility of guaranteeing to the underprivileged and sometimes unemployable person, a minimum guaranteed income because, in a sense, they may be casualties of prevailing labor conditions or prevailing economic conditions.

Chapter 6

HOUSING IN THE NEW ERA

With the growth in population, the crowding of people in the cities, the obsolescence of existing housing, and the desire of people to regain some of the personal contact lost in urbanization of communities, the housing situation has become replete with a multitude of problems, not the least of which is economic. The problem of housing is host to a multitude of others, such as the adequacy of educational facilities, discrimination among shifting racial and ethnic groups, inadequate governmental facilities and the increased cost of same and the adequacy of public utilities available.

It has been said that there are over half-a-million substandard housing units in the United States. The cost of single housing units has risen to over $20,000 and it is estimated that over 70% of Americans cannot afford to purchase a home without governmental assistance. The federal government has taken some steps to relieve the financial burdens of providing housing. States such as New York enlarged the state's right to take property by eminent domain, to permit it to develop larger housing facilities. The state has also been permitted by legislation to ignore restrictive local zoning regulations. The feeling is that satellite communities should be developed to house the city's growing population outside the central city. Restrictive zoning regulations which grew out of snobbery in many suburbs have been successfully challenged in an increasing number of cases.

Courts have played an important part in the protection of certain low-income groups. A landlord, for instance, was barred from collecting overdue rental where code violations were known by him to exist in the housing, the court holding the lease to be void. A court prevented eviction of a tenant who had reported violations of the housing code. There has recently been drafted a Model Residential Landlord-Tenant Code by the American Bar Foundation which suggests changes in the present landlord and tenant laws. Among other things, it would prevent the recovery of rent by slumlords who do not maintain the premises in good order.

If you purchased a home in the past, you were -- and still are -- pretty well bound to the terms of the written agreement and you could not look outside of the writing. In California recently, a court held that a bank could be held liable in negligence if it financed the construction of private houses which were defectively constructed, or if there was thin capitalization by the builder and this was known to the bank. Thin capitalization creates the risk of cutting corners. The courts are more and more putting aside the old theory of caveat emptor (let the buyer beware) and imposing a duty of due care on those involved.

Other advances in the housing field may be noted. Often, when new housing is started, many of the old inhabitants of the buildings to be torn down to make way for the new, are out in the cold without a home, unable or ineligible to afford housing in the new and unable, in any event, to wait until the new is built. Since 1968, several courts have recognized the standing of these displaced persons to sue and the courts have found that a justiciable issue exists (a justiciable issue is one which may be tried by the courts). Some federal housing programs now require that displaced persons be provided with replacement quarters.

Public housing, with 100% financing has become very attractive but some communities have fought it as ghetto construction on a higher scale. Nevertheless, public housing, in infinite variety, is increasingly cited as the answer to the housing crisis which exists in most cities today. It is expensive and will require optimum cooperation between the federal, state and local authorities as well as the general public.

Coupled with the financial problems of housing is the fact that without control, available space would soon be used up for housing. Many states have set up commissions calculated to preserve areas for other purposes -- such as recreation centers, parks, bird sanctuaries and so forth.

Much of the above does not affect the average person who owns his own home, or leases from a private owner of property either an apartment or a home. The incidents of a lease remain largely unchanged at this time.

Leases

Most states require that leases for a period of more than one year be in writing. While the relationship of landlord and tenant may arise without a writing, as in tenancies at will, sufferance or weekly, monthly or yearly, most leases are reduced to writing. Most states have laws regulating the amount of notice to be given by a landlord to a tenant he wishes to have vacate the premises, in the absence of a lease.

A written lease contains the basic elements of the agreement between the parties -- description of the property, names of the parties, the duration of the lease, the amount of rent to be paid and in what installments, and under what conditions the premises are rented as well as the conditions under which the tenancy terminates. There is a large body of law governing the relationship of landlord and tenant and for this reason, all important aspects of the renting should be spelled out in the lease. If a lease is silent, rent is not due until the expiration of the period or term; the landlord pays real estate taxes and water bills if the lease is silent; a tenant may not assign or sublet without the landlord's consent unless the lease says so.

The tenant has the right of possession without interference by the landlord or others acting on his behalf. The right to possession is valid against the whole world, except for such limited purposes as the lease may provide. The lease may limit the right to possession by specifying the purposes to which the premises may be put; the tenant may not use the premises illegally and if he does, the lease is terminated. Stated affirmatively, a tenant may use the premises for any legal purpose, unless restricted by the lease, so long as he does not damage the property or change the premises substantially.

A tenant has the right and generally the duty to occupy the premises, i.e., enter into possession, so that they will not be subject to fire hazards which are a threat to unoccupied premises. A tenant is relieved of the obligation to pay rent if the premises become uninhabitable through no fault of his own. Many states have specific laws granting a tenant this relief. A building may be rendered uninhabitable for many reasons -- fire, rat infestation, lack of heat when equipment is under landlord's control.

A landlord who fails to make repairs may be subject to liability to his tenant and their guests but he is also in many states subject to criminal sanctions. In some states, the tenant may make the repairs and deduct the cost from his rent.

The most important single duty under the lease, at least to the landlord, is the duty to pay rent. Rent may in some cases, if specified in the lease, include real estate taxes and other charges against the property but this is not customary in leases of residential property. Security posted with the landlord for tenant's performance under the lease, is considered a trust fund and the landlord is required to treat it as such. He is not supposed to mix it with his personal funds nor may he use it. In New York, he is supposed to deposit it in a bank account and to notify the tenant of the name of the bank.

A tenant should notify the landlord of the need for repairs and of any adverse proceedings against the property.

If a tenant fails to pay rent or to perform any other duties under the lease, the landlord may sue to recover the premises and for damages occasioned by the tenant's failure.

Where it exists, rent control may impose certain restrictions on the parties to a lease, primarily as to the amount which may be charged as rent but also as to accommodations.

The Purchase of a Home

The most important purchase the average man will make is that of a home. The steps involved are outlined below simply for information. The purchase or sale of real property is extremely complicated and the procedure is beset with dangers to the unwary. To consummate the purchase or sale of real property requires the cooperation of four or five different groups: 1) the present owner, 2) his attorney, 3) the purchaser, 4) his attorney, 5) the bank or other lending institution or its attorney, 6) the title company which will be required to insure the marketability of the title.

The first formal document involved in a sale of real property is the contract. Sometimes an informal binder is signed by a prospective buyer, but care should be taken to avoid this; for a binder, if it complies with the requirements of a contract, may be construed to be a contract. The contract contains the precise

32

description of the property, the terms and conditions upon which it is being sold, the rights and easements against the property, provisions as to how rents, and charges against the property shall be apportioned between the parties; that the title shall be marketable; the form of the deed to be given by the seller; the title company which is to insure the title; how payment is to be made, and many other things. Stated briefly, the contract controls the rights and obligations of the buyer and seller. It must be in writing, of course.

Usually there is a lapse of at least one month between the time the contract is signed and the deed executed to the new owner. This is to allow time for a number of things to be done. The buyer is probably going to have to arrange for financing of mortgage; the title company must search the records to determine if the seller has good title, whether the taxes are paid, if there are any liens against the property and many other factors. The lawyers will prepare the instruments of sale and, if there is to be a mortgage, the attorney for the bank will probably prepare the instruments required.

At the time of title closing, or the transfer of the property from the seller to the buyer, taxes, water charges, insurance premiums, fuel, rent and other credits and charges are prorated between the parties or apportioned. For example, if at the time of the closing of title, a paid tax bill covers a six months period, of which four are past, the seller is entitled to get one third of the amount paid from the purchaser. If, on the other hand, the bill is unpaid, the seller would have to pay 2/3 of the bill to the buyer. After the transaction is completed, the attorneys for the parties will send their clients statements of the financial transaction -- these are known as closing statements. The deed is sent to the Register's Office to be recorded in accordance with the law.

Condominiums and Cooperatives

Because of the high cost of real property and services, and the urbanization of communities which makes less space available for building, two new forms of property ownership have been developed in recent years.

33

Condominium literally means joint ownership but more descriptively, it refers to a unit in a multi-unit dwelling; each of the residents is known as a unit owner; he enjoys exclusive ownership of his individual apartment or unit, holding a fee simple title to it (this is the same type of ownership that a person who owns his own home generally has), while retaining an undivided interest, with all the other condominium owners, in the common facilities and areas of the building and the grounds which are used in common by all the residents of the building or buildings.

A cooperative apartment house is one in which each resident has an interest in the entity, usually a corporation owning the building, like shares of stock in the corporate cooperative owner, and a lease entitling him to occupy a particular apartment within the building.

Both of these forms of cooperative ventures in real estate have gained greatly in popularity for the reasons defined above. In the condominium, the resident has exclusive title to his own apartment and shares title to the rest of the premises with the other residents. In the second (i.e., cooperative) the resident has shares of stock or other evidence of interest in the corporation which has title to the premises and a lease entitling him to occupy a specific apartment within the building or buildings.

Mobile Homes

Evidence of the resourcefulness of man in the housing field is the development of the popularity of the mobile home. Originally, and still today to a limited extent, the mobile home was on wheels, free to move about, capable at least of being transported from site to site. In time, however, many homes became very ornate and quite stationary, with permanent plumbing and sophisticated fixtures. Taking a page from the book of prefabricators, standardization has helped make production more reasonable in cost than most conventional stationary homes.

The mobile home, of whatever size or shape, has become a pleasure vehicle in that it is a novel and adaptable vehicle for traveling and vacations. As leisure and population increased, the traveling public popularized its use. The mobile home has a versatility that pleases many age groups, so it is safe to say that it will continue to grow in popularity. Its appeal originally was to young married couples and retired persons with time and a little money. As population places a greater burden on available housing it may well be that many more will answer their housing needs by acquiring mobile homes.

As indicated above, mobile homes now come in a great variety as to size and luxuriousness, and the prices accommodate purses of different capacities. A mobile home has been defined as not being a house and therefore runs into zoning law difficulties. It cannot be placed in an area zoned for single houses. It is a home where the homeowner does not own the ground on which it stands, even though permanently stationed.

Mobile homes have been treated differently in different localities with respect to taxes. Also, there is little consistency in their treatment by the zoning authorities. Undoubtedly, tax treatment and zoning regulations will become standardized in time. More mobile home parks will be developed. Taxation will become more equitable. Local prejudice against the mobile home will undoubtedly diminish as the mobile home parks become less of an eyesore than they have been in some localities. Paradoxical as it may seem, the mobile home is here to stay and will probably contribute greatly to the solution of the housing problem that is so critical at the present time in the United States.

Chapter 7

CONSUMERISM

Consumerism is a relatively new term which perhaps more than anything implies protection of the consumer. It is further evidence of process of reexamination and reevaluation of institutions and processes of our society. It is a force which seeks to counterbalance the power of corporate power which for many years has been motivated solely by profit. This force for change is fostered not only by the private consumer but also by the very corporate powers which in large degree necessitated the development of consumerism. The need for consumer protection has sparked the public's interest and is now a serious social concern. Many champions of the consumer have appeared on the scene and his rights are being asserted in the courts and in the legislative forums.

Foremost among them is Ralph Nader (and "Nader's Raiders" who number in the 100's) who for five years has been stirring the public conscience. Out of their actions have come many reports, books, television programs, testimony at Congressional and administrative hearings, law suits, petitions, letters to the government and corporations. Campaigns to organize college students in a consumer crusade have also been conducted. Many changes have been effected by Nader and his groups -- tough air pollution laws, significant consumer protection legislation, review of pesticides, safety of motor vehicles. Nader also spurred government agencies like F.T.C. and I.C.C. to long overdue reforms. Nader and his raiders have become ombudsmen -- watch dogs of the people -- even against their own government. It is an example for those who despair of getting any reforms or changes in a society which some feel has become a mammoth corporate beast. Three years ago Nader established a Center for the Study of Responsive Law where half a dozen senior raiders work. There is also a Center for Auto Safety, a Center for Law and Social Policy, and a Project for Corporate Responsibility.

The consumer's right to be given the facts he needs to make an informed selection or decision has so often been stated as to make it an accepted part of our philosophy. In spite of this assertion, the truth is that the consumer is ill-informed or misinformed at every point and the difficulties of correcting this condition are almost unsurmountable. Modern advertising, a thriving business, artifically contrives many of the consumer wants. There are many who assert that the net effect of the great amount of advertising is that man is slowly being alienated from his environment and from reality and being introduced to the world of fantasy. The advertisers maintain that man's personality is fixed at an early age and all that advertising does is to reflect the values already existing in that person or the society similarly conditioned. The question may become -- can we legislate a revolution in social values or must we wait until the system changes under its own force or destroys itself?

Of course, most advertising is completely irrelevant to the merits of the products advertised. Appeals are made to masculinity, femaleness, to snob appeal created by the fact or representation that the product is used by a famous person. False claims by advertisers are not the major problem today. These can easily be reached by existing laws. More damaging is the fact that advertisers omit reference to the most relevant facts, as well as dwell on totally irrelevant romantic facts. Thus interest rates or cost of a loan are now required to be disclosed. Advertising by concerned groups, such as the government private agencies, are used to counteract the effect of producer's advertising. For example, the heart and cancer organizations have had television spots showing the ill-effect of smoking to dispel the romantic pictures painted of green glades and manly men. Banning advertising altogether is also a method of combatting misinformation (smoking advertisements are now banned on television).

Another form of control may occur at the time the sale of the product is offered. At that point, the producer is in some cases now required to show clearly the quantity of the commodity as well as the price. Standardization of packaging is also a means of keeping consumers informed but this is not in general practice.

But quantity is not the only thing to be measured in order to assess the value of a product. Quality determinations are exceedingly difficult to make and to enforce. How can you rate the quality of different loaves of bread? Grading has been suggested as a means of showing the relative qualities of different products. This has been done with meats to a limited degree. The problem of grading is beset with difficulties. Apart from differences in tastes, the vastness of the organization required to do the grading, and the policing of the grading and the persons encharged with it would make it an incredibly difficult and costly procedure.

Nevertheless, progress is being made in parts of the field of consumerism. Education of the consumer is of prime significance. The dissemination of information is growing. For example, three items are being offered by the President's Committee on Consumer Interests -- "Speak up, when you buy a car", "Be sure before you sign", and "Knock, Knock".

Consumer research is not a very new thing. The Consumers Union which was preceded by Consumers Research, is an organization owned and controlled by consumers which brand test products. It publishes a consumer guide, which contains no advertising; it buys its products on the open market; its personnel are not permitted to have any connections which would affect their judgment. Its unbiased reports give a consumer a basis for making an independent choice before entering the store; they stress safety rather than style; they tend to improve products by pinpointing defects or flaws; favorable ratings increase sale of the more meritorious products. The Consumer Union reports are helpful but of limited use since they reach the middle class, educated persons and not the poor or those most apt to be exploited in the market place.

Consumerism is still in its infancy. It is limited to the narrow areas of fraud, safety in use of products and a few others. It is likely that before long, it will extend to collateral areas, such as environmental hazards of certain products; pollutant effect on man, even in the form of television programs.

There are certain rights which have crystallized over the years. A consumer has the right to expect a product to be safe for his use. He has the right to have a product to be what it is represented to be. He has the right to know what he is getting into (for example, what he is paying for credit). A consumer has the right of privacy. Today, huge networks of credit agencies collect personal data and rumors about persons seeking credit and pass them off as fact to others in credit organizations. This is most insidious because the person about whom such "facts" are collected may never know what misinformation is being spread about him and may have his reputation or credit, at least, destroyed before he can do anything about it.

Today, a person receiving unsolicited merchandise need not even return it. This is one small step forward in handling the unwarranted advances of advertisers. Unsolicited and lost credit cards have been a headache and laws are now being enacted to protect the consumer, at least limiting the potential liability of a credit card holder.

Insurance policies which are so abstruse that even lawyers are sometimes hard put to understand them have also been subjected to criticism and the actions of insurance companies in arbitrarily cutting off automobile insurance or refusing to renew without cause are subject to criticism.

Transportation safety has been very much in the foreground. Ralph Nader has become a household word in this field. The National Highway Safety Bureau lists three categories of auto safety -- passing ability, braking distance, and tire reserve-load capacity. Certificates must be supplied with each vehicle sold after January 1, 1970. Other categories of safety features and standards for them will undoubtedly be added.

The National Highway Safety Bureau has also made investigations and brought pressure to bear on auto manufacturers to notify consumers of defects in vehicles and to recall the vehicles, if necessary.

The federal government, through various agencies, has set other standards of safety. The Federal Aviation Authorities set standards for aircrafts and flying schools and related matters; the Coast Guard conducts search and rescue missions to be sure but they also keep marine waters from getting polluted, they keep mariners from dangerous waters, they approve equipment using the waters, they conduct public education programs; and a variety of other related subjects.

Many have said that a lot of our headaches in the field of consumerism have arisen from the reality that massive economic power has passed into the hands of giant corporations and today scientific and technological expertise is linked to this power and is engaged in creating new products rather than investigating the hazards of all products. In a sense, it is claimed that science has been prostituted to the profit motive.

Harvey W. Wiley, the father of Pure Food and Drug Legislation, said many years ago that the right of the consumer is the first thing to be considered and would be worth more in this country than the actual protection of health or the freedom from fault. The theme of all legislation of this kind is the same -- no matter what its name might be, whether pure food, regulation of the public utilities or restraint of predatory corporations -- the right of the individual citizen against monopoly and corporation. Much later, the matter is stated as follows: The crucial question is, can science and technology, harnessed to the engine of the corporate giants designed primarily to make money, provide the new kind of knowledge needed? He further states that past experience indicates that it cannot; that there is a need for new mechanisms to generate new, unbiased, scientific information useful to all. A great economist once said that consumption is the sole end of all production and the interest of the producer ought to be attended only so far as it may be necessary for promoting that of the consumer.

It has been suggested that testing of products be done by an independent agency which would occupy a role something comparable to that occupied by the certified public accountant. Such an agency could certify to quality and safety of products. This appears to be headed in the direction of independent investigation and reliability of information upon which the consumer may rely.

There appears to be general agreement that many steps are necessary. The facts of the neglect of the consumer are appalling. Many thousands are killed on the highway, many killed and disabled because of a product's lack of safety, many individuals are victimized because of their lack of knowledge. The nation is being polluted with more than industrial waste, smog, gas fumes, oil slicks and garbage; billions of dollars of poorly constructed and designed merchandise, shoddy goods and dangerous products flood the markets. Freedom of enterprise and individual freedom, the policy of allowing a producer free range, thus keeping a consumer uninformed, have defined a path which may lead to national self-destruction.

Several national programs have been instituted to assist the consumer. The Uniform Consumer Credit Code was approved by the National Conference of Commissioners on Uniform State Laws. A National Consumer Law was drafted by the National Consumer

Law Center, an office of Economic Opportunity, a funded project at Boston University. Both are under consideration by the various states. Both completely revise the consumer credit laws of the states. Both require disclosure of the annual rates and dollar finance charges. Both require a single writing to cover the transaction. Both prohibit the signing in blank of document of credit. Maximum rates are set forth to cover various types of credit accounts. Certain types of agreements are prohibited by both. Among these, are confession of judgment, in which case the borrower or debtor agrees that he owes the money when he negotiates the loan; the use of negotiable instruments to evidence the debt. Such instruments may be transferred to innocent parties against whom the debtor will not be able to assert defenses he had against the person who sold him the merchandise or lent him the money. Among the other prohibitions, are that the assignee cannot be freed from defenses which a debtor may assert against the original creditor; assignment of wages are also prohibited; waiver of any rights under the acts is also prohibited; and many other devices formerly used by creditors are also prohibited under the provisions of these acts.

If adopted, either of these acts will go a long way to protect a purchaser of goods on time or a borrower of money.

It is predictable that with the new awareness not only of the general public but of the legislators and judiciary, many more beneficial actions will be taken to protect the consumer.

Chapter 8

CREDIT WITH CAUTION

Credit has become so intrinsic a part of our way of life, that it is almost impossible to transact any business or even engage in social activities without using it. Credit and its uses and abuses have been under considerable scrutiny primarily because the average person does not really know how much his use of credit is costing him. There are many types of credit devices, which are briefly described below.

Charge Accounts

Charge accounts in the nature of revolving accounts should be used judiciously. Unpaid balances on such charge accounts are payable in most instances with interest. Interest on unpaid balances usually runs to about 18% a year, which is far in excess of interest payable on a bank loan. Credit cards and installment contract purchases may also carry this interest rate. Most persons do not realize what the interest rate is on a purchase made under these circumstances. To counteract the average person's ignorance of rate of interest and other charges on time purchases and loans, many states have passed what are generally referred to as "Truth-in-Lending" legislation. These laws require the lender to state the rate of interest, the dollar amount of interest and other charges.

Secured Debts

Secured debts are those where something or someone else's credit is used to secure payment of the obligation of the debtor. There are various types of secured debts. The pledge is perhaps one of the oldest and simplest means of securing a debt. The debtor delivers to the creditor an object or thing of value as security for the debtor's repayment of the primary obligation. The creditor retains the object until the debt has been repaid. Ownership of the property pledged remains in the debtor but it may be lost if he does not pay his debt. If the creditor is obliged to sell it to recoup the amount of the loan, and realizes more from the sale of the object than the amount of the debt, he is obliged to remit the balance to the debtor. If the sale yields less than the amount of the debt, the debtor is liable for the balance, and he may be sued for it.

Some things pledged are too unwieldy or cannot be delivered physically to the lender. In such cases, the borrower delivers to the creditor evidence of title or right of possession (for example, bills of lading).

Chattel Mortgage

A chattel mortgage is another form of security for a debt. In this case, the lender transfers title to the borrower, and upon payment of the debt, the lien which the lender has is discharged or satisfied. In the event of non-payment title passes to the lender. Possession remains in the borrower until he fails to make the payment required of him. The chattel mortgage and the conditional sales agreement are both devices used to purchase personal property on an installment basis. Both of these types of sales are required to be documented and in general must be filed with the appropriate authorities or they are not binding as to third parties who do not know of the transactions.

A conditional sale differs from a chattel mortgage in that title stays in the seller until the buyer or debtor has completed his payment for it. The buyer has the right to possession and has possession in both types of purchases. A person buying on a chattel mortgage basis gets title to it as well as possession but the title and possession can be taken away from him if he fails to make payment. One who buys on a conditional sales basis gets merely the right to possession until he makes payment, at which time he acquires title.

Real Estate Mortgage

The real estate mortgage follows the same pattern as the chattel mortgage. A real estate mortgage may be used for many purposes including the purchase of a home, home repairs or as security for a loan unrelated to the premises. It is most often used in the purchase of a home by the average person, who secures a bank loan to enable him to make the purchase. Title is in the buyer (mortgagor) who borrows money from a bank (mortgagee); the buyer has the right to possession, the right to receive the rents and other income from the property. In the event of a default on the part of the buyer, a formal costly procedure must be followed -- foreclosure. There are many special laws which control a foreclosure proceeding, especially if the property foreclosed is the home of the debtor. When a mortgage is paid off, the bank or other creditor executes a satisfaction of mortgage, which indicates that the debt has been paid in full and that the creditor releases the property from the lien of the mortgage. A satisfaction mortgage must be filed in the appropriate recording office; otherwise there is no record of the discharge of the debt and the property will be considered as having a lien against it. The satisfaction of mortgage must be filed in the county where the property is located.

Guaranty and Suretyship

These devices involve the use of one person's credit to secure the debt of another. In other words, a guarantor states that if the original debtor does not pay a debt, he will. A guarantor differs from a surety in that the surety is liable on the debt along with the original debtor and the creditor may look to either of them for payment at the time it is due. The law requires that all instruments of this sort which involve the undertaking by one person to answer for the debts of another must be in writing.

Negotiable Instruments

While negotiable instruments are not strictly speaking credit devices, in the ordinary sense of the words, they are formal documents involving the exchange of goods or money. They may be transferred or negotiated. There are many types of negotiable instruments. A promissory note is an unconditional promise to pay on demand or at a specified time, a sum certain. A draft is an unconditional order to a third party to pay at a time certain, or on demand, a fixed amount to the bearer of the order. A check is a draft drawn on a bank and payable on demand. These instruments may be transferred -- or negotiated -- from one person to another by endorsement. A person may so endorse a check as to prevent its further negotiation. For example, if you endorse your pay check, "For deposit only -- to the account of _____", it can only be deposited to your account. Limiting words of this sort can effectively prevent the check from being endorsed by a stranger and cashed.

A negotiable instrument has been defined as a written instrument, signed by the person making it and containing an unconditional promise or order to pay a sum certain in money payable on demand or at a specified time, and payable either to the bearer or to his order. It includes a draft, a check, a certificate of deposit (which is a receipt from a bank with a duty to return it) and a note. An instrument may start out as a negotiable instrument and lose its negotiability by an endorsement placed on it, as described above. Negotiable instruments are also known as commercial paper.

Any discussion of credit should include some reference to usury. Lending money at a rate greater than the maximum permitted by law is usury. The law makes a distinction between legal and lawful rates of interest. The legal rate of interest is the amount which may be charged if no rate of interest is specified. The lawful rate of interest is the highest rate which may be charged by agreement. Charging more than the lawful rate constitutes usury. This is very easy to state but much more difficult of application. Many creditors may add charges which the law may construe to be, in fact, interest. If these charges added to the amount specified as interest, make the interest rate higher than the lawful rate of interest, then it would be considered usury.

Relief of Debtors

A person who has become insolvent (that is -- is unable to pay his debts) may in most states call together his creditors and seek to persuade them to accept part payment in full settlement of his debts, upon surrender of his property to them. If they all agree, the debtor may be discharged from his obligations. Insolvency may be voluntary, in which case the debtor starts the proceedings. The Federal Bankruptcy Act gives an insolvent debtor a chance to start fresh. Originally, the term "bankrupt" meant a trader who hid himself or did other acts calculated to cheat his creditors out of their money. Today, a bankrupt is an insolvent person or one who otherwise fits the definitions under the National Bankruptcy Act. A person may commit an act of bankruptcy which under the law permits his creditors to bring proceedings to have him declared a bankrupt, even though he may have assets of value. Bankruptcy laws permit the marshalling of the assets of the bankrupt and the discharge of the debts which he may have. In the absence of fraud or illegal transfers of property and upon compliance with the law, a person discharged in bankruptcy is free of his debts.

Fair Credit Reporting Act

Under this newly enacted federal legislation, users of credit will be able to challenge the accuracy of adverse reports on their credit standing, and may seek correction of errors. Thus, a person turned down for consumer credit, insurance or employment because of an adverse report must be notified of the fact and given the name and address of the credit bureau or other investigative agency that compiled the report. At the consumer's request, the reporting agency must disclose to him the "nature and substance" of all information in his file, except for medical information. Any erroneous information must be corrected. If an item is disputed, the consumer may give his side in a written statement that must be included in his file and in reports to merchants, insurance companies and employers.

This legislation, together with the "Truth-in-Lending" laws represent a beginning toward protecting the consumer on credit.

Chapter 9

PROTECTING LIFE AND PROPERTY

Insurance is a broad and technical field and little more than definition can be attempted here. An insurance policy is a most complicated legal document. It is somewhat anomalous that the average policy holder knows little about his policy except what his insurance broker tells him. The broker gets his commission from the premium paid to the insurance company but is considered the agent of the insured (casualty insurance). An insurance agent, on the other hand, is an agent of the company (life insurance).

The business of insurance is closely regulated by law and standards and rates are set by the insurance authorities of the states for many types of insurance policies, such as fire and automobile.

To determine the needs of the family for life insurance, many facts should be considered, such as the age of the children, their educational status, whether they will be attending college and at what time; what the parents' wages are, what the family assets consist of, what other assets will become available and at what time -- these are a few of the facts to be considered.

Life Insurance

Life insurance is probably the most important insurance to a family. Life insurance differs from other types of insurance in that it protects only against the occurrence of death, an event certain for all of us. Other types of insurance generally protect against the occurrence of an event which may not and hopefully will not occur -- such as fire, theft, injury or liability. There are several types of life insurance policies available which fulfill different aims.

Term insurance. Here, the insured is covered for a specified time period only; if he should die within this period, payment of a stated sum will be paid to the beneficiary he names or

47

to his estate. No loans are permitted against this type of life insurance policy as it has no cash value.

Limited payment life insurance. Payment of premium is for a definite period of time but insurance continues for the full period specified, generally the life of the insured.

Ordinary life insurance. In this type of insurance, a premium is generally payable until death; however, dividends accumulating on the policy are applicable to the payment of premiums.

Endowment. Payment of premiums is continued for a definite period of years, as indicated in the policy, at the end of which period, the principal sum is paid to the insured; in the meantime, he has had life insurance payable to his beneficiaries, if he does not survive for the period specified.

Annuities. Annuities are really a form of retirement insurance. Generally, annuities do not have life insurance features, but some policies provide for some life insurance features. Annuities generally guarantee a life income to the beneficiary or another named by him at the maturity of the policy.

Generally, life insurance policies provide for a "grace" period. A grace period prevents forfeiture of the policy for non-payment of premium if payment is made after the due date but within the stated period of grace.

Most life insurance policies have a cash surrender value -- that is, they may be borrowed against. Most life insurance policies may be reinstated within a stated period of time, upon payment of back premiums and interest. Misstatement of age no longer invalidates the policy but permits adjustment of amounts payable under the policy, geared to what would have been the correct premium at the correct age.

Rights of beneficiaries. If an insured person does not retain the right to change the beneficiary, the beneficiary acquires an absolute right to the proceeds. If the insured does have the right to change the beneficiary, he is said to be the owner of the policy and the policy is treated as his property. As his property, its cash value can be reached by creditors, but the death proceeds cannot. If an insured wants to change the beneficiary on a life insurance policy, he must do this during his lifetime. He cannot do so by his will because the rights of the beneficiary will have matured at the death of the insured, the death being the event upon which the policy proceeds are payable. Where a policy is payable to a spouse, later divorced, payment will still be made to that person unless changed by the owner of the policy. However, a person who murders another whose life is insured in the murder's favor, will not be allowed to profit from his own wrongdoing and will not be permitted to recover under the policy on the victim's life.

Where a beneficiary and an insured die in the same accident, so that it cannot be known who died first, it will be presumed that the insured survived and the proceeds go to the insured's estate unless he has designated an alternate beneficiary, in which case the proceeds would go to that person.

Life insurance is increasingly being used in family savings and estate planning. Purchases of life insurance reached an all-time high in 1969, totalling over $1.3 trillion dollars. Because of the rising cost of living, some companies have been experimenting with policies in which payment is being geared to the increase in cost of living.

Americans bought nearly $159 billion during 1969, an increase of $8.1 billion over 1968. Annuities continue to grow in use, the greatest growth being in group plans, as a type of pension plan. The number of Americans with insured pension plans reached 10 million during the 1969 year.

People buy life insurance for a variety of reasons but the most important reason continues to be to provide financial security and protection for their families when they die. A person adds to or creates an estate upon the purchase of life insurance. He protects the future of that estate as he maintains the policy over the years.

Casualty and Liability Insurance

Literally, all insurance other than life insurance is casualty insurance. In the insurance business, however, different terms have been adopted to refer to different types of casualty insurance.

Accident insurance. This is insurance against personal injury or death resulting from accidental means. The premium varies according to the risks involved in the employment of the insured. The premium is naturally higher for hazardous occupations or activities. Generally there is no recovery permitted if the insured intentionally caused the death or injury. This involves a determination of what is "accidental". If a person drives a car carelessly and is injured as a result of his own negligence, he will nevertheless be permitted to recover under the policy because it is an accident within the meaning of the law. If he commits suicide or intentionally cuts his arm, it is not an accident. The test may be whether he intended the results of his act. But an eminent jurist has said that an attempt to distinguish between accidental means and accidental ends plunges us into a bog.

Accident insurance indemnifies against loss of time, expenses and suffering resulting from an accident which causes physical injury. This is usually done by the payment of a fixed sum on a weekly basis. It often includes payments to heirs if the insured dies as a result of accident.

Fire insurance. Fire insurance, as its name indicates, protects against fire and indemnifies against losses occurring to the property protected by the policy. The fire causing the loss must be of hostile origin. A fire policy specifies the nature of and location of the property insured. It usually contains an extended coverage clause which extends the protection to damage caused by wind storms, hurricanes and similar catastrophes.

There is no liability under a fire insurance policy where the insured misrepresented the use of the building, or is guilty of other material fraud. Generally, there are exclusions from fires caused as a result of enemy attacks, insurrections or other political violence. If the premises are vacant for more than a certain number of days, unless otherwise stated, there is no coverage. Fire insurance coverage may be cancelled only on adequate notice to the insured.

In the event of a fire, the insured is required to take appropriate action to protect the property against further damage and against theft. He is also required to give timely notice, as set forth in the policy, to the insurance company. Disagreements as to the amount of damages are required to be submitted to an appraiser. The insurer has the option of taking all or part of the damaged property at the agreed appraisal value or repair or re-place it within a reasonable period of time.

If the premises insured are a place of business, the owner or insured is required to maintain an inventory in a safe place (safe from fire) so that it will be available in the event of a fire.

In the case of a fire, the damages under the policy may not exceed the actual value of the property or the cost of repair or replacement. If there are several policies in effect, the loss is prorated among them, according to the face amount of the policies. This is known as "contribution". If the insured is underinsured and does not carry insurance equal to at least 80% of the value of the property, the insured bears a portion of the loss. This is known as "co-insurance". If there is total destruction, the principle of co-insurance does not apply.

Automobile insurance. Automobile insurance has become a number one headache to automobile owners and drivers, and possibly, also to insurance companies. Cases involving automobile accidents crowd the court calendars and the costs not only to automobile owners and drivers but to the state are approaching the astronomical. Everyone agrees that something has to be done about it. More and more persons take the view that vehicular accidents are an incident of our society and should be treated as a socio-economic problem. There has been an increasing acceptance of the "no fault" automobile insurance plan. The subject has been hotly argued in many forums. Some jurisdictions have adopted it (i.e., Puerto Rico, Massachusetts), but it is too early to evaluate its merit. The cost of the insurance will not necessarily go down for the policy holder. At this time, there is much agitation in New York for the passage of no-fault automobile insurance legislation. Many factors favor the adoption of this type of policy. Among them are the escalating cost of automobile insurance; the practice of insurance companies to cancel out insurance or to fail to renew it without specified or relevant reason; refusal of companies to accept certain risks, forcing a policy holder to seek insurance from an insurance pool where the rates are higher. Legislation has been proposed to compel the insurance company to state reasons for cancellation or refusal to renew. But this does not cure the problem for the policyholder who has been refused insurance.

Insurance rates differ depending on whether the vehicle is used for business or pleasure, the value of the car or vehicle and many other factors. Generally, for years, a spouse could not recover in an action against her husband if she was a passenger in the car he was driving. This principle is being reexamined and in some states recovery is permitted. Some states exclude from protection all members of a family under a liability policy of this nature.

Automobile insurance includes many types of insurance that are not considered liability insurance. Collision insurance, for example, protects the owner of a vehicle against damages to his own car, even though he may be at fault and would be barred from recovery against the other driver on the latter's liability policy. The liability clause may permit recovery for the full amount of the loss or for the full amount less a stated sum to be deducted. This is called the deductible. Most cars have fire and theft insurance for their cars and medical payments for passengers. The premiums vary with the amount of coverage. In all types of automobile insurance, payment is made to the insured or the person standing in his shoes on the happening of the contingency giving rise to right of indemnification.

There are a number of other types of insurance available to protect against almost anything. One of the most useful is a consolidation of several policies -- it is the homeowners' policy which combines in one policy the features of fire insurance, extended coverage, insurance against theft and burglary, and liability insurance for injuries sustained by third parties on the premises of the insured.

Another branch of insurance is often required or at least desirable in the conduct of a business. Fidelity insurance covers persons who are entrusted with money in the course of the performance of their duties. These are bonds, payable upon defalcation of persons who violate their positions of trust. Trustees and guardians, bank employees, executors and administrators and other persons in positions of trust are frequently required to be bonded. Guaranty insurance insures the performance of agreements such as builders' contracts and is simply a means of measuring what non performance would cost the person to whom the bond is payable if the contractor fails to perform within the specified period of time.

Insurance companies own a great portion of the wealth of this country. It has been said that the insurance codes of this country are in great need of revision. Many states have set up legislative committees to study the industry, not without considerable resistance from the insurance industry. It is predictable that such studies will be made and much needed reform will follow, including the possibility of a federal government initiative in the field.

Insurance, then, is another area where many changes may be expected in the next decade, particularly with respect to the automobile insurance industry. There is pending in New York a bill to regulate the insurance companies in some respects. Among the complaints of policy holders are the following.

Cancellation of policy without any fault on the part of the policy holder and with no reason given for the cancellation. In one instance it turned out that the insurance company had dumped the broker who placed the policy; in other cases, the insurance company decided not to insure within a certain area where the insured happened to be living.

A bill introduced in New York would prevent cancellation of homeowner's policy and similar policies except for nonpyament of premiums or change in use of premises that increases the risk, or acts of the insured that have increased the risk. Another would prevent non-renewals of auto policies, except for loss of license, non-payment of premium or fraud. Another would require the insurance company to give 90 days notice of cancellation rather than the 45 day notice now given. Another would give a policy holder the right to appeal a non-renewal and reinstatement of his policy if his appeal succeeded. Another, as noted, would require the insurance company to give reason for cancellation or failure to renew.

This is only a small beginning. It seems rather strange that a business as rich as the insurance business has the right to eliminate all losers, suggesting, as has been done, that the government insure the losers, eliminating the risks for which insurance companies have been paid over the years. It is a fair statement to say that the insurance business is invested with a public interest and the government could regulate the "grand dame" a lot more closely than it has in the past.

The greatest outcry for reform of the insurance business has been, as indicated above, with respect to the automobile insurance industry. Many, many questions remain to be answered. Why is the cost of insurance so high? Why is it so difficult for some drivers to obtain insurance? Why are some required to go to the "pool" (assigned risk) and pay higher rates? The complaints fall into two classes -- the availability of insurance and the cost of it. Availability becomes increasingly important as almost all states require insurance and condition the issuance of an auto registration upon presentation of proof of insurance.

Reform is necessary for additional reasons. The congestion of the courts is in great part attributable to the heavy load of automobile negligence cases. This not only delays trials of automobile cases, but delays the trial of other cases, and otherwise thwarts the proper administration of justice in our courts.

Chapter 10

DEATH AND TAXES

Death is a traumatic experience for everyone but it can also be financial disaster for a bereaved family. A family man must face the fact that he will probably die before his wife. A woman lives about 5 years longer than a man her age and most women are several years younger than their husbands. This means that she will survive her husband by 7 or 8 or more years. She will have to take care of the family, not only without his guidance but without his earning power. It is important to plan the family finances with this in mind.

Consideration should be given to social security payments and other benefits which accrue at the time of the death of the wage earner, such as life insurance proceeds, pension payments and similar benefits, which might be said to stand in the place of his wages. Consideration should also be given to other assets which may have been accumulated by the family over the years, such as savings accounts, securities and other interests in property. Another factor to consider is the status of the home -- is the home owned outright? is there a mortgage outstanding against it? The personal status of each family member is still another important factor. The ages of the children, their educational status, the ability of the surviving spouse to earn a living, the ability of children to contribute to the family income and similar facts should be weighed in establishing a family plan.

In the event of death, there are several ways in which property may pass from the dead person to his heirs. Property may pass by operation of law or by contract. Usually, property passes by operation of the laws of succession or by a will of the original owner, or a combination of both. Everything a person owns at the moment of death is included in his estate, for the purpose of distribution by the laws of descent and distribution or by will.

Certain property, however, is not owned and therefore not included in the estate. A life insurance policy which by its terms names another as the owner (who may also be the beneficiary) is not part of the estate. Death is simply the event which activates the payment to be made and sets the terms for such payment. This is also true of joint bank accounts, joint home ownership and other property held jointly by the deceased and another person.

The Will

There have been many examples of cases where no will was left by a husband which fact caused great hardship to the family, either because there were minor children for whom guardians had to be appointed or management of the estate was placed by law in the hands of the least competent person; or disposition of the property was by law, which frustrated the real purposes of the deceased. By making a will, executed with appropriate formality, and in compliance with the requirements of the laws of the state in which he is domiciled, a man assures the desired disposition of his property.

The right to dispose of property at death is a right granted by the law. In the distant past, this right was limited. In feudal England, for example, real property passed to the eldest son, to the exclusion of other children and to male children in preference to females. This is, of course, no longer true. But the right to dispose of property by will is still limited in a few respects. For example, in most states, a husband or wife cannot cut off the other by will. This subject will be discussed in more detail later.

A will should in most cases make a complete disposition of all property possessed by the testator, which does not pass by insurance or right of survivorship. A will should take into consideration various contingencies, such as the possibility that a man's wife might not survive him, or that children will be born after the execution of the will or the death of the father, or that property bequeathed to specific persons might not exist at the time of the death of the testator, or that the person to whom a gift is made might not survive the testator. These examples are given simply to point out the complexity of the facts which might affect the terms of a will. A will is certainly not a do-it-yourself project but requires the expertise of an attorney.

Inheritance without a Will

If a person fails to make a will, the law provides the disposition which should be made of the property. The staturory disposition follows the normal pattern of human affection and con - cern. In general the wife and the children are the prime beneficiaries.

Real property descends according to the law of the state in which it is located. Personal property descends according to the law of the state in which the decedent was domiciled at the time of his death. Title to real property passes immediately to the beneficiary when the decedent dies while personal property goes to the representative of the estate and through such person to the ultimate beneficiary. The representative of the estate is either the Executor (or Executrix, if a woman) of the will or the Administrator (Administratix, if a woman) if there is no will.

The estate of a deceased person is liable for his debts and bequests made by him may be set aside if there are not enough assets in his estate to pay for his debts. Assets may be sold to satisfy debts he made during his lifetime.

Rights of Spouse

A husband or a wife cannot, even by will, cut off a surviving spouse. They are said, today, to have a "right of election" against the will. The right of election derives from common law rights of dower and curtesy, limited rights in the deceased spouse's real property, which have benn abolished in most states in favor of the broader right of election. Neither the old curtesy or dower rights nor the modern election against a will can be destroyed unilaterally (that is, by one spouse, acting alone). The right of election varies from state to state, some following the common law rights rather closely but extending the right to personal property as well; some giving a full life estate. The right of election must be exercised within a specified period or may be lost.

Persons entitled to take in the absence of a will are indicated in the statute of the state of which the decedent was a domiciliary or where the real property was located. Persons entitled to take are listed in order in which they take; if there are no members of the preceding class or kin, the estate goes to the next class of beneficiaries. If no relatives can be found, the property goes to the state (escheats to the state).

The question is often raised as to what happens when a husband and wife die in the same accident at approximately the same time. This has caused problems in the past, necessitating in some instances medical proof as to the exact time of death of each. A law has been passed which simplifies things somewhat. The Uniform Simultaneous Death Act has been adopted and is in effect in 46 states. It provides that where two persons die as a result of a common accident and it cannot be ascertained which died first, each estate will be disposed of as if each decedent has survived the other, and is disposed of in accordance with his will or by the laws of the state, if he had no will.

In a number of states, there exists what is known as community property. Under this system, any property acquired by the husband or wife during the marriage is considered to be the property of both in which each has an equal share. On the death of either, the spouse who survives gets one half of the entire community property, the rest being disposed of according to will or by the laws of the state.

Effect of Divorce, Separation or Annulment on the Right of a Person to Inherit from His Spouse

Since a divorce terminates the marriage, divorced persons lose the right to inherit from their spouses. Where there has been a separation between the parties, unless it is coupled with abandonment by the surviving spouse, the rights to inherit are not affected. An annulment, however, which vitiates the marriage from the start also defeats the rights to inherit.

The husband and wife who are separated may release their rights to inherit from the other spouse.

Administration of Estates of Persons Dying without a Will

When a person dies without a will, it is usually necessary that a person be selected to administer the assets of the deceased person. The administrator or administratix is appointed on application to the court. The persons entitled to be appointed are specified in the applicable statutes, which establish the priorities among various eligible persons. If the estate consists of property, all of which is exempt, it may be possible to avoid administration of the estate.

Certain persons are not eligible to become administrators of the estate. Among them are minors, under 21, felons (persons convicted of felonies), aliens, illiterate persons, and other persons who would not qualify to occupy this position of trust.

A petition is filed for the appointment of the administrator with notice to all persons interested in the disposition of the estate. An administrator is required to file a bond covering the estimated value of the estate and to guarantee the faithful performance of the duties of his office.

An administrator has the duty to collect the assets of the estate, including debts, prepare an inventory of assets; pay all debts, giving creditors appropriate notice to present claims within specified period; obtain tax waivers to permit transfer of assets to the administrator, thus permitting him to take possession; to file inventory; appoint appraiser if necessary to evaluate assets of the estate; to distribute the assets as required by law and to render an accounting of his actions.

Special provisions exist in most states for the disposition of small estates, which either provide for the avoidance of administration or the simplification of the procedure applicable to small estates. Generally, small estates are defined by setting a dollar limit on the value of the estate which can be classed as small.

Inheritance When There Is a Will

Any person of sound mind, over the age of 21, may make a will as to real and personal property. In some states, a minor over 18 may make a will as to his personal property. Married minors are emancipated and in most states may make a will as if they were 21 or over.

A testator must be competent to make a will. This has to do with mental capacity to understand and intend the act of making a will. Age does not bear on competency. A person of advanced years may be just as competent to make a will as any person in the prime of life. A person may become incompetent after he executes a will but the test is whether he was competent at the

59

time he made the will. At common law, aliens could not dispose of property by will but this is not the case in the United States today. Even during war years, property of enemy aliens was held by the Office of Alien Property Custodian and much of the property has since been turned over to the designated beneficiaries.

As indicated elsewhere, there are limitations on the power to dispose of property by will. In most cases a person cannot entirely disinherit his spouse. Except for Louisiana, a parent may disinherit his children.

Execution of a Will

After preliminary discussions and conferences, an attorney prepares a will which is then ready for execution. A will must be executed in the presence of a specified number of witnesses who sign in each other's presence and in the presence of the testator and so declare. The testator in their presence declares the document he signs to be his last will and testament. Care should be taken to select witnesses who are younger in years, and whom you have known for some time. It should be remembered that a witness to a will cannot receive more under the will that he witnessed than he would have received if there had been no will. Most states require two witnesses to the execution of the will but the prudent attorney has the will signed by three to take care of the possibility of death or disappearance of one or more of the witnesses.

A will should be kept in a safe place, either in your attorney's office or in your safe deposit box. The disadvantage of keeping it in a safe deposit box is that the safe deposit box of a decedent is automatically closed upon his death and a court order is required to open it. A will may be changed in several ways but the best way to do it is to execute another will with the express provisions that all prior wills are thereby revoked. Sometimes a will is revoked in part at least by events which take place after its execution. Marriage may operate to revoke provisions so that a surviving wife would be taken care of. Children born after execution of a will may inherit under its terms, thus changing the amounts of bequests to others. Where the subject of a specific gift ceases to exist, the legacy is revoked.

A will may be changed by a codicil. A codicil is in the nature of an amendment to the original will and modified it only to the matters referred to in the codicil. A codicil must be executed with all the formality and in as strict compliance with the law as the original will.

A word should be said about certain unique wills which do not have to comply with the strict requirements of the law, or are not executed with the usual formality. Generally speaking these should be avoided if at all possible.

A handful of states allow for probate wills which do not comply with the usual formal requirements. The holographic will is one written entirely by hand of the testator and signed by him.

A non-cupative will is an unwritten will by a soldier or sailor in active military service, or a mariner while at sea, in immediate peril of death or last illness. In most instances, the will becomes invalid if the testator survives for longer than the period specified in the statutes. Also, a non-cupative will is generally invalid except as to small amounts of money. Three witnesses to the testator's declaration are generally required.

Probate of a Will

In the administration of an estate where the testator left a will, the executors take the place of the administrators. The first step is to probate or "prove" the will. This requires the witnesses to the will to appear in the appropriate court and testify to the facts of the execution of the will. The procedure has been simplified in some states so that it is no longer necessary for a witness to appear in court but an affidavit setting forth the pertinent facts is acceptable.

After the will has been proved, the person named as executor in the will takes charge of the assets of the estate and in general performs the duties described above as those of the administrator. He, too, pays out assets, bills, distributes the estate and performs such other duties as the will might require. If the executor is a close friend or a trusted colleague, it is customary to dispense with the bond by the terms of the will. This results in saving to the estate.

Anatomical Gifts

In this day of organ transplant, it becomes increasingly important to make such a gift, if contemplated, in time so that it may be properly utilized. Here is one point at which the medical and legal fields overlap. Many questions arise in connection with organ transplants. It is generally acknowledged that an anatomical gift should be voluntary. However, questions arise as to how voluntary a gift is when made under family pressure or when made by inmates of penal institutions. What about a gift from a minor who is healthy? How does one handle post-mortem gifts? Which member of the family has the right to decide whether transplant from a deceased person shall be allowed? Also, and perhaps the most serious question of all, just when does death occur when an organ transplant of the heart is contemplated? Traditionally, death has been defined by doctors as the moment at which it can first be declared that the heart, lungs, and brain have all ceased irreversibly to function. There is some argument for redefining death as the moment when just one of these organs ceases to function. Body tissues of organs designated for transplant must be moved after death of the person but before the death of the tissues or organ designated for transplant. If the transplant is not done within this limited period of time, the transplant will fail, at least in part. While it is clearly wrong to do anything to hasten death, it has been argued that it is almost as wrong to delay pronouncement of death unnecessarily when such delay might result in a failure of the transplant and death to a person who could have lived with the transplant.

TAXATION

Taxation has been called the art of so plucking the goose as to procure the most feathers with the least possible amount of hissing. There are many who claim that the hissing is growing loud, particularly among the great body of middle-class Americans. Taxing hurts and limits activities of the individual and makes many despair of the power to plan their own lives. It has been said that the power to tax is the power to destroy. It is at least inevitable that inequities result from any system of taxation because it is in the nature of some men to try to avoid payment of taxes. Justice Musumanno, a Pennsylvania jurist, said that where there is an income tax, the just man will pay more and the unjust man will pay less on the same income.

On the other side of the fence is the truism that taxes are the life blood of the government, or, as Holmes has said, the price we pay for civilization. Certainly, no government could exist without taxes.

Taxes come in all sizes and shapes: income taxes, real property taxes, inheritance and estate taxes, gift taxes, sales and use taxes; cigarette and excise taxes, alcoholic beverages taxes, stamp taxes, gasoline taxes, highway use taxes, utilities taxes, unemployment insurance taxes, mortgage recording tax, franchise taxes, unincorporated business tax, special city taxes and hidden taxes; licenses and registration fees, to name only a few.

No attempt will be made here to define all the taxes or even to list them exhaustively. Charts V and VI show the prevailing state income taxes and sales taxes which are the taxes of which most of us are aware.

Tax reform is a subject of recurrent interest. It is long overdue at this time but reform in this field comes slowly and over the protests of those who have found loopholes in it or whose special interests are benefited by existing tax law.

The most onerous of all taxes in America is the federal income tax. There has been a greater clamor, and hissing, if you will, for many years for the reform of the federal income tax, to spread the burden of taxation more equitably. The Tax Reform Act of 1969 undertook to do this. While it fell short of expectations, it did effect some reforms.

The federal income tax is a progressive tax in that the rate of taxation increases. In addition to the basic tax, there is a temporary surcharge tax which was 10%, but which reduced to 2 1/2% for 1970 and 1971.

Among the changes made in the federal income laws are the following.

Changes Affecting Individual Tax Rates

The personal and dependency exemption will be increased from $600 to $750 by 1973. The percentage standard deduction is increased gradually over a three year period as follows: in 1971, it will be the lower of 13% of adjusted gross income or $1,500. In 1972, it will be the lower of 14% or $2,000. In 1973, it will be the lower of 15% of adjusted gross income or $2,500.

A low income allowance removes many poverty level taxpayers from the tax rolls.

A new maximum tax rate of 50% is set on earned income starting in 1972.

A new tax schedule is provided for single taxpayers with lower tax rates. A new tax schedule is also provided for heads of household which falls between the rates for singles and married couples. Tax rates for married couples are unchanged.

One does not have to file if single if income is $1,700 or less (or $2,300 if you are over 65); if married no filing required if combined income is under $2,300; if over 65, if income is under $2,900; if both spouses are over 65, there is no need to file if combined income does not exceed $3,500. Anyone claiming a tax refund must file regardless of income.

Changes Affecting Capital Gains and Losses

A number of changes, to take effect over a three year period, will make capital gains and losses less attractive to the taxpayer. In other words, the treatment of capital gains and losses will be less favorable. At the end of the three year period, the tax on capital gains will reach 35%. But the 25% capital gains tax which has been in effect for many years will continue to be effective as to $50,000 of an individual's capital gains. Several other changes were made in respect of capital gains and losses.

Changes Affecting Employees

Moving expenses are now deductible by employees, even those who are self employed. Employees receiving stock in lieu of earnings will lose some of the benefits (as to time of taxability -- deferred compensation) previously attached to such transactions.

The Tax Reform Act of 1969 restricts the permissible activities of foundations by imposing taxes on business activities. A foundation which deals with itself (self-dealing), or which fails to distribute its income for the exempt purposes for which it was formed or has extensive holdings in unrelated business enterprises, or makes investments which jeopardize its exempt purposes, or engages in lobbying or other activities seeking to influence legislation will lose tax benefits.

An excise tax of 4% is now imposed on a foundation's net investment income. An income tax may be imposed on the termination of the foundation's exempt status. Net investment income is gross investment income less expenses paid or incurred in earning the gross investment income.

Self-dealing relates to activities of foundations with persons such as a member of family establishing the foundation, government officials, substantial contributors, foundation managers.

Foundations have been tax favored devices, generally formed for commendable purposes, but in some instances used to hide income or split it in such a fashion as to avoid the full impact of taxation.

Charitable Deductions

Deductions to charitable organizations have been increased from 30% to 50% of an individual's net adjusted gross income.

Depreciation of Real Property

New depreciation rate rules have been put into effect to plug up still another loophole in the tax structure.

Depletion Allowances

Some reductions have been made in depletion allowances but the reductions are quite negligible. Oil and gas wells' depletion

rate is reduced from 27 1/2% to 22%; sulphur and uranium mines'
rate goes from 23% to 22%; other depletion percentages remain
unchanged. (For gold and silver the rate remains 15%.)

Farm and Hobby Losses

These constituted another tax shelter and have been affected by the 1969 Act. Now the tax law provides for the recap-
ture of these losses from other income of the individual and in
other respects tightens the hobby loss provisions. The background of this is the regard the law had for the farmer's problems. Many high bracket taxpayers recognized this as a good
thing and went into farming as a sideline. The raising of cattle
and development of citrus fruit trees are two well known examples. For a number of years, there would be little income from
the projects, but expenses would be deducted from ordinary income. When it came time to sell the cattle, the sale would be
treated as one of capital goods and a capital gain would be real-
ized. Capital gains were taxed at a much lower level (it used to
be 25%) instead of at income level which generally runs very much
higher.

This tax shelter has been destroyed because, now, proceeds from the sale of the farm will be taxed as ordinary income,
to the extent that the post 1969 tax losses due to the farm were
used to offset non-farm-tax income. A number of other similar
steps have been taken to shut off this avenue of taxable income
escape.

Corporations and Shareholders

The Act takes many steps to eliminate tax benefits from
operating a business through many or multiple corporations, by
treating the group as one. The multi-corporation was a device
for income splitting. Treating the group as one, it is entitled to
only one $25,000 surtax, one $100,000 accumulated earning credit
and it is restricted in other respects. Again, the ultimate result
will be achieved gradually over the next several years.

Federal income taxation is an area which will undoubtedly
receive a continuing amount of attention. Many of the loopholes
which started with quite commendable reasons for their existence

66

have outlived their original usefulness and have become weapons of inequity. Time has eradicated some of the reasons for their existence, but the exemptions continue to exist, either because of neglect or the selfish lobbying of interested groups. Exemptions rooted in long past socio-economic conditions, or in the self-serving operations of a few, have no reason for existence in a democracy and may in fact be working to the detriment of our society. In the final analysis, they may destroy the goose that lays the golden egg. A serious reexamination of the principles of taxation and its implications in the present society and economy is a matter of prime importance today.

PART III

NEW LIFE STYLE AND SOCIETY

Chapter 11

PUBLIC WELFARE

One of the most controversial issues facing America today is that of public welfare. The basis for the controversy lies in a conflict of the two underlying theories of welfare. One is based on the belief that public assistance is a matter of right and the other rests on the belief that public welfare is a mere privilege or the act of generosity on the part of the state to its members in need. This difference in philosophy manifests itself in the attitude of the states towards welfare. If the welfare client has a right to the aid which he receives (on the theory that he is entitled to share in the wealth of the country or is a victim of society), he has an enforcible property right in welfare funds. If welfare is considered a gift from the sovereign state, the state has the right to impose conditions and limitations upon the receipt of the gift. Historically, the latter view is the basis for most of our welfare laws. Based upon this theory, it is not unreasonable that a welfare client should be required to take a loyalty oath, that he should register for employment, that he should make a disclosure of his assets and permit an investigation of his financial situation and an inspection of his premises.

There is nothing in the United States Constitution which guarantees the right to welfare or the right to freedom from poverty. Nothing in the Constitution guarantees more than the opportunity to achieve these ends.

Many states provide for the aid and care of the needy. This does not mean that the state necessarily recognizes welfare as a right. It may mean that the state considers it an appropriate function of government to take care of its needs and impinge upon the rights of the taxpaying public to do so.

Law is an expression of the social conscience. Conscience changes and with it -- not in point of time, but flowing from it -- the law changes. Whatever the history may have been, the fact is that, today, public assistance is looked upon as a right of a

71

citizen. Many states put top limits upon the amounts which a person may receive as public assistance but even setting such limits has been challenged as unconstitutional.

Welfare payments have been growing at an increasing rate. Today, they are quite staggering. In 1968, the average expenditure for assistance in the United States was $20.55 per person. Out of every $1000 of personal income, $6.60 went to public assistance. An average of about 50% of this aid came from federal funds but this ratio varied greatly from state to state. In New York, for example, an average of $61.90 was spent each year per inhabitant; only 39% came from federal funds, and one out of every eight persons was receiving assistance.

Aid to families with dependent children also varies greatly from state to state. Average monthly payments run about $40 per month in Mississippi but are about $254 in New York. This is due to two factors -- one, that Mississippi has a lower cost of living and, two, that Mississippi has a lower scale of living. The cost of living in Mississippi is so much lower than in New York that what would give a recipient of welfare a comfortable living in Mississippi would be a pittance in New York, where the cost of living is extremely high and housing facilities are taxed to the limit and where even non-welfare clients find it hard to make ends meet.

In New York, where the cost of public welfare has reached mammoth proportions, legislation is being considered which would permit the authorities to send an applicant back to his home town, whether in or out of New York, and to pay the fare back. An earlier law which applied only to persons coming from out of state was declared unconstitutional.

All states have aid to dependents programs for the needy. These general assistance programs are operated without federal funds. A number of programs are federally funded and to some extent controlled. Aid to dependent children, aid to the blind, disability assistance, old-age assistance are aspects of the federal programs.

There is a system of grants-in-aid from the federal government to the states set up under the Social Security Act for needy persons who are permanently and totally disabled because of various kinds of physical and mental disabilities. A few states have special assistance programs of their own. While old-age assistance programs are in effect generally, the shift is to old-age insurance. The philosophy is that a person who has contributed to society during his productive years should be provided for in his old age.

What is needy differs from state to state but a common test is that a person has insufficient funds or other resources to provide reasonable subsistence compatible with decency and health. Another test is that resources be sufficient to rpovide a "reasonable standard of health and well-being." A few states set up standards in terms of specific income. All states set limits on assets which an applicant for old age assistance may own and still be entitled to assistance. Some states reserve the right to collect the amount of benefits from the estate of the person assisted.

One important new development in the welfare field in recent years is a work incentive program which allows a recipient of public assistance to have a portion of his earned income and work expenses deducted from his earned income in figuring the amount of a grant of public assistance. Residence requirements which used to be the rule as far as state aid was concerned were declared unconstitutional by the United States Supreme Court. However, the pendulum may be swinging the other way as states find themselves in financial straits. Governor Rockefeller of New York has asked the Legislature to enact a law providing one-way fares for persons not meeting the residence requirements of the locality. This applies to all persons, including citizens of New York. An earlier law which limited this requirement to persons coming from out of the state was the law referred to above and was held unconstitutional.

In line with the newer philosophy, to preserve a man's dignity even though he is receiving public assistance, new federal regulations require states to separate determination of financial eligibility from provision of social services and instituting a declaration system rather than an investigatory system. In many states, only a declaration of need is necessary to accompany an application for welfare assistance. No independent investigation is made.

Another program of special significance is one which originated in 1960. A food stamp program was initiated for low income families. Under this program free food stamps are provided for eligible families. The applicant goes to a bank and upon the payment of a certain sum receives a much larger sum of food stamps which he then presents to his grocer in lieu of money after he has shopped.

In spite of all the benefits, or perhaps because of them, many persons have expressed dissatisfaction with the present public assistance program and reforms have been suggested. Among them are the following:

The present system should be scrapped for one providing benefits to all persons below the poverty level who are in need and should embrace national standards of public welfare adjusted periodically to the cost of living.

There should be work incentives, including exemption of some earned income and a full program of training and work with opportunities for public service when the private sector of society cannot provide the same.

Eligibility determination should be simple and administered with regard to the dignity of the needy persons.

The concept of a guaranteed minimum income is gaining support. There is at the present time a Commission to Study Income Maintenance which would be in a position to establish guidelines for minimum income levels.

Some of the dissatisfaction with the welfare picture comes not from the administrators of welfare nor from the welfare clients but from the taxpayer, particularly the middle income taxpayer who feels his living has been seriously affected by the heavy welfare burden, and his incentive seriously affected because, with little or no effort, he would still be supported by society. Upon analysis however, this may well turn out to be an attack upon the tax structure which places the heaviest burden on this segment of the population.

There is no doubt that the problem of welfare is a big one, and a costly one. When it is considered that 72 out of every 1000 persons were assisted in New York State (1 out of 8 in New York City); 82 out of every 1000 in Puerto Rico; 85 out of every 1000 in Louisiana and Mississippi, the magnitude of the problem becomes apparent.

Legal aid to the poor is now recognized as essential to their well-being and in the best interests of society. Many volunteer and neighborhood agencies have sprung up for the purpose of protecting the poor in court and to represent them in legal matters for what is justice if it cannot be activated for the poorest among us.

Chapter 12

MAN AND HIS ENVIRONMENT

The expansion of man's activities has resulted in a massive drain upon the environment of air, water and living things, compelling them to serve both as a source of supplies and a dumping ground for the waste generated by man's activities. Having disrupted the ecological balance, or the ability of nature to renew itself, man now is compelled to rehabilitate or restore nature. If he fails in this, he may well have failed himself as well. The problem is that to restore nature to its original state is impossible. Simply by removing causes that disrupted it will not restore it. Too much has been done to it. The clock cannot be turned back. Technology of the most sophisticated sort will have to be employed in an attempt to remedy the situation. It has been said that what is needed is a drastic and immediate evaluation of the relationship of man to his environment. What is more important? That we continue to build highways and giant electrical plants or that the world ceases to exist? All the giant plants in the world would be forever silent if life could not continue to exist on this planet. The ruins of the world might well be criss-crossed with interlocking highways packed with vehicles whose mufflers are muted and whose motors ceased to purr. A civilization or culture has been created in the last several decades different from anything that went on before -- with a built-in capacity to destroy itself. If we fail to reverse the course that man has set on, human reason itself will have failed and human life might well cease to exist.

Population Explosion

Population explosion, which affects the future ability of the world to feed and sustain its inhabitants, has been tackled on several grounds. Poverty and the conditions of the disadvantaged members of society are getting more and more attention and many programs, governmental and private, have been developed to ease these conditions. A great spate of commissions and other groups have sprung into action in an effort to cope with the disorders of society. Groups of concerned citizens, realizing the delay or inertia of the law, have taken up the cudgel in various fields.

Population has increased at an alarming rate. In 1650, the world's population was 500 million; by 1850, it had doubled; by 1930, eighty years later, it had again doubled to 2 billion; by 1970, it was nearly 4 billion, or twice that it had been only 40 years earlier. The interval of time within which it doubles keeps getting shorter. The projection is that in 1000 years, every particle of earth, inside as well as on the surface, would be covered by human beings.

Although the United States has only 6% of the world's population, it consumes about 30% of the world goods and unrenewable resources. This is an effective answer to those who claim that there is alot of room in the United States.

Results of overpopulation are well known: malnutrition or starvation; antisocial behavior; environmental pollution; increasing costs to all segments of society.

Many solutions, some very drastic and inimical to our present philosophy, have been proposed. Among them are the repeal of all laws limiting advertising of birth control devices or medicines; or abortions, or sterilizations; the subsidizing of contraception, sterilization, and abortion by bearing the cost of these practices; cash payments to individuals who will undergo sterilization; payment of subsidies to women of child-bearing age if they desist from having children; removal of tax exemptions for children after the first two children; elimination of tax disadvantages which single taxpayers bear; raising the age at which one may marry; allocating funds for research on contraception, sterilization and abortion; legalizing homosexuality; providing legal and tax framework for family or group units not based on parent-child relationships. Compulsory methods have also been suggested -- which would include the necessity for a woman to have a license to have (at most 2) children; requiring women to use contraceptives; compulsory abortions, sterilization and infanticides. These are drastic and alien to our thinking and are a long, long way into the future and probably will only be resorted to as a last desperate measure.

Pollution of the Environment

The second Earth Day was celebrated on March 21, 1971. Such events do nothing more than to publicize the concern some members of society have about our environment and direct at-ptention to the immediacy of the problem. It is a small step towards education and, hopefully, responsive action.

One of the most distressing problems confronting the world today is pollution of the environment. To say that this is one problem is a gross understatement and minimizes greatly the enormity of the crimes committed and permitted against the environment to the possible permanent detriment of the world.

Air Pollution

There are a number of pollutants so lethal in effect that to permit any amount is criminal negligence, it is claimed. For such pollutants the only remedy is the immediate discontinuance of their use. This is not too simple since the pollutants may be the backbone of an industry and to stop their use would mean economic disaster not only to the industry but to the many persons who may be employed by it. However, there really is no choice in these cases, according to experts, if survival is to be achieved. In a situation such as this, the only remedy is to discontinue the use immediately and relocate -- or compensate -- those affected by the action. This example is cited simply to demonstrate the complexity of the problems which are created when a remedial step has to be taken.

Many factors contribute to air pollution -- people, geography, weather. Most significant of all are people and their activities over the last 200 years. Electric power and its manufacture; the automobile and its widespread use; the simple fact that more people are leaving the rural area and concentrating in the urban centers -- all these facts tend to aggravate the seriousness of the situation.

It has been said that the single most deleterious factor in air pollution is the process of combustion. This is so significant a process of modern life that at our present level of technology automobiles could not be operated without it, electricity could not be produced, homes could not be heated, and industry would be helpless without power created by it. These facts complicate immeasurably the problem of eliminating sources of air pollution.

Air pollution is particularly bad in the northeast section of the country. Coupling the great quantity of emissions from many engines with adverse weather conditions, such as inversion of the atmosphere, or geographic conditions such as deep valleys which hold lethal gases prisoner, results in a dangerous, and sometimes deadly, situation.

While smoke is the most visible pollutant, it accounts for only 10% of the pollutants; the balance consists of poisonous gases, one half of which are the deadly, colorless, odorless carbon monoxide gases. Carbon monoxide issues from the exhausts of countless motor vehicles at an alarming rate. But these are not the only deadly gases to come out of the exhaust pipes. What makes the emissions even more dangerous than when they are in their natural states is what happens to them when they hit adverse weather conditions. They have been responsible not only for the terrible smogs for which a number of cities have acquired a dubious reputation but for the many casualties in life and health and much property damage.

The effect of air pollution on human longevity and health are well known. Many persons suffering from respiratory diseases did not survive the disaster at Donora, Pennsylvania in 1948; nor the deadly smogs of New York and Los Angeles, at other times. Emphysema is on the rise and even the well person suffers from chest pains and eye irritation. Many pollutants contain cancer producing agents. With the barrage of evidence, there can no longer be any question of the threat which air pollution poses.

To state some of the causes and effects of air pollution is only a small part of the matter. In the past the control of such matters was left to the local governmental units -- such as the town and county and city. Today, these activities continue at an accelerating pace but more and more air pollution is becoming the concern of the states and of the federal government. Air knows no boundary lines and knowledge acquired by one agency could well be utilized by another. There are now numerous agencies concerned with the problem, but some degree of coordination of efforts has been effected by federal legislation.

The first federal air pollution program was established in 1955. This basically authorized research and study of the problems

78

involved. In 1960, a study was authorized, and made, as to the effects of motor vehicles exhaust emissions on human health. The Clean Air Act of 1963 was the beginning of active regulation by the federal government, the earlier programs being specifically study programs. The present federal law is the Air Quality Control Act of 1967, amended in 1970. Under this act, while the states are responsible for taking remedial action to correct undesirable conditions of the air, the federal government can step in and correct the condition if the states do not. Under this law, the federal administrator is directed to identify pollutants and set standards of tolerance and related matters for all air pollution factors. The states are required to submit plans for remedying the conditions, for approval to the federal administrator. If the plans are found inadequate, the administrator sets forth supplementary state plans. The act is federally enforced, on notice to the violators and the state. He may take action to force compliance, if notice fails. The federal administrator is empowered to take direct action if the state fails or if an emergency condition exists.

Part of the federal program is to make grants to support training programs at universities and at local government level. The federal government makes air surveys, evaluates national emission standards and the impact of pollution control on the economy of the communities involved.

The federal government has also issued automobile and diesel emission levels for 1970 model vehicles. Gasoline additives are required to be registered. Federal approval is also required of all exhaustion control systems but regulation of this requirement is left to the individual states.

A major part of federal funds will be directed towards the creation of interstate regional air shed agencies which will set up standards for the states.

The states have also taken independent action. Over half the states have established programs in an attempt to control air pollution.

Another action on the part of the federal government has been to require contractors working on public contracts to meet requirements for pollution control; in the event they fail to do so, they may be penalized but, and perhaps this is more effective, they may be barred from getting public works contracts.

This whole area has become characterized by increasing litigation, and one can expect, over the next few years, a growing case law that will interpret recent legislation.

Water Pollution

The pollution of the rivers, lakes and coastal regions and oceans does not only affect the health of the people but poses a real threat to the continued existence of the world itself. Increased population and industrialization have placed heavy burdens on the water supply (which is said to remain constant). It is estimated that by 1980, we will need twice as much water as we now need. If more and more water becomes polluted, the remaining untainted water will fall far short of being able to take care of the needs of the people. Undoubtedly what is needed is a reevaluation of allocation of water to the various purposes it serves.

Since the supply of water is limited, one way of handling the water problem is to treat waters so that they will be reusable. Standards have been set by all states. Many states have adopted water pollution control laws. The federal government has set up standards of water control for the states. Treatment of waste is required in connection with the federal program. Also, water users may be required to treat waste before discharging it, to remove nutrients in order to inhibit the growth of algae.

Water pollution control is somewhat complicated by the historic rights of persons on whose lands the waters are located or which waters have been appropriated by landowners. Some of these rights have been recognized for centuries. Since waters generally do not respect property lines, a doctrine evolved that allowed a person to use water in a reasonable manner, so as not to destroy or render useless or materially diminish the application of the water by other persons owning land through which the stream ran. These are known as riparian rights. The rights of a riparian owner include the right not to have the water contaminated or polluted. The first water pollution case in New York was brought in 1868. There a dairy farmer got an injuction to prevent an upstream owner from polluting the water with the waste from a cheese plant and pig farm. In 1877, the City of Rochester was enjoined from discharging waste into a stream. In 1913, the New York courts went even further. They enjoined a pulp mill operator, employing hundreds of persons (an operation valued at over a million dollars), from discharging wood wastes into a stream, impairing the purity of a stream. The plaintiff in that case sustained very minimal damages. The principle of this case, where little damage had to be shown to get an injunction against an offender, has not been followed very closely in later cases but it is still good law in New York and could be used to achieve some of the purposes of water pollution control.

The state of New York is one of the earliest states to take measures to protect the water supply. Legislation was enacted as early as 1906 but the first really comprehenisve act was passed in 1949. By that act, a Water Pollution Control Board was established and was directed to set up a program for the solution of the problem of water pollution within the state. Later, this board was replaced by the Water Resources Commission which is an independent body. In 1965, the Pure Waters Program Law was passed. The Water Resources Commission has the power to classify waters and adopt standards of purity. The enforcement of the program is left to the Department of Health. Waters are classified on the basis of "best use" ranging from drinking water, bathing, fishing, industrial, agricultural and waste disposal. This relates to surface waters. A system of classification for ground waters is presently being developed. In New York, there is a permit system which prevents new sources of pollution. No new disposal system may be constructed without a permit from the Department of Health. The act also makes it illegal to discharge any undesirable material into classified waters. The provisions of the law are enforcible by injunction, fines, penalties and criminal prosecution. This program is not intended to limit methods of controlling water pollution and other programs have been instituted.

Water pollution is an area where the maximum degree of cooperation between the states and the federal government is necessary. This need has been recognized by the formation of the Association of State and Interstate Water Pollution Control Administrators of all state and interstate agencies.

New York, in response to the Federal Water Quality Control Act, submitted its classifications and standards and after some changes they were approved by the federal agency.

81

Thermal Pollution

Thermal pollution is a type of water pollution which results from the excessive heating of the water which in turn disturbs the natural balance (for example, destroys fish in water). New York state, recognizing the damage that can be wrought by disturbing the natural temperature of waters, introduced new thermal pollution control regulations. The greatest producers of thermal pollution are generator plants, which use water for cooling purposes. Nuclear plants are particularly offensive.

Effects of thermal pollution are very grave; increases in water temperature increase growth of algae, change the taste and color and odor of water; cold blooded fish life is also threatened by extreme changes in temperature; decrease in oxygen supply to fish; supply of cooling water for industry is diminished.

Corrective action for thermal pollution is readily available by legislation and education.

Noise Pollution

Noise is another by-product of our highly complex and industrialized society. Attempts to control noise have not been very successful. Nor are they very new. Zoning regulations were to a certain extent designed to keep noises away from residentail sections of a community. As we become more crowded, as in - dustry grows, the places free from the growing cacaphony diminish in number.

Noise has been looked upon as a nuisance we can learn to live with, but doctors have branded it as a health hazard. Excessive noise causes hearing losses. (It has been pointed out that the average grown person in America has hearing comparable to that of an eighty year old in remote areas of the Himalayas.) This hearing loss is not just psychical but real cell damage. Noise can cause physiological changes and affect the heart, the glands and respiratory systems. Noise can obscure warning systems or impair communication at times when danger exists. The problem was the subject of consideration of the National Conference on Noise as a Public Health Hazard. The first such conference was held in 1969. It is a beginning and hopes are that it will not only educate the public to the realization that noise constitutes a health hazard but accelerate action seeking to abate noises.

The ultimate question is can man reclaim his environment? Can he rehabilitate the natural resources he has laid waste and restore the sweet sound of silence to the universe?

The crimes against our ecology have been characterized as dwarfing into insignificance the problem of crime in the streets in terms of the destruction of life and property. It will take the combined vigilance and action of our courts and lawmakers and those who police the laws to effect significant changes.

Chapter 13

CIVIL LIBERTY AND HUMAN RIGHTS

No discussion of new life style and its impact on the law would be complete without reference to increasing protection for the fundamental rights of persons guaranteed under our system of government. In the period 1948-1968, the advancement of these rights was a major test of the legal structure of our society. While progress has been formidable, it has not been fast enough for many, with the result that, among certain groups, particularly minority ethnic and racial groups, there has been an increasing trend toward action, as distinguished from law, as a tool in the effort to eliminate patterns of discrimination and deprivation of rights. This action-oriented approach has increased tension within American life.

The civil rights movement in the United States had its origin in the Declaration of Independence which states that "...(A)ll men are created equal, ...they are endowed...with certain inalienable rights, ...among them are Life, Liberty and the Pursuit of Happiness...."

A liberal application of the comprehensive principles set forth above might well have saved this country a lot of heartache and conflict over the years that have passed since the enunciation of these principles.

The first ten amendments to the Constitution of the United States are known as the "Bill of Rights." To a certain extent, they give specificity to the principles declared to be the rights of all men. Either by specific language of the amendment or by court interpretation, the "Bill of Rights" was found to guarantee rights only as against the federal government. This is understandable when seen against the backdrop of history. The individual states were very zealous in protecting their own identity against any government other than their own. They feared that the federal government might usurp the power of the states to regulate and govern themselves.

84

To insure protection of citizens against state action, the States adopted provisions similar to the federal provisions in their own State Constitutions. But it was not until the passage of the 14th Amendment that the United States Constitution protected the individual against actions of the States. The Constitution does not protect individuals against other individuals unless rights are violated under color of law.

The terms "civil liberties" and "civil rights" have been distinguished from each other on the basis of the person or agency against whom they are enforceable. Civil liberties are said to be those liberties which the government (federal or state) may not infringe. In other words, civil liberties are those which protect an individual against improper government action. In effect, civil liberties define the treatment any individual has a right to receive from the government. It might be said that the bill of rights specifies the conditions under which individuals consent to be governed.

Civil liberties include, among other things, freedom of religion, separation of church and state, freedom of speech, freedom of the press, the rights of free assembly and of petition to the government, protection against double jeopardy, against unreasonable search and seizure, and excessive fines and punishment, the right against self-incrimination, the right to counsel in criminal cases, the right to trial by jury; the right to bear arms.

The Bill of Rights specifically provides that the enumeration of the rights in the Bill shall not be construed to deny or disparage other rights held by the people. The Bill also specifies that any rights not delegated to the United States by the Constitution nor prohibited by it to the States are reserved to the States or to the people.

These broad philosophical rights may vary from state to state and within the federal system. Like all philosophical concepts, the contents differ in interpretation depending on the person or court interpreting the same. Nor are they absolute in the sense that there are no limitations on their exercise or penalties attached to their exercise. Defamation laws limit free speech. You may say what you will but if you damage a person's reputation, you may find yourself sued for libel or slander. You may write a book and may find yourself criminally liable for violating obscenity laws. But the fact that there are limits on the exercise of a right does not deny the right but rather underscores its existence. The

85

content of that right may vary with changing mores or life styles, if you will, but the right continues to exist.

Civil rights have been defined as the protection one person has against the acts of another. They are much more difficult to enforce because they involve interpersonal relationships, which may not be defined at all or are difficult to define, or involve conflicts of individual rights. They can be enforced only by enacting laws, specifically designed to correct an evil (such as discrimination in housing), adopting constitutional amendments (for example, granting women the right to vote) or litigation interpreting existing law to cover factual situations as they develop. Much of the development of civil rights can be attributed to private law suits or private groups such as the National Association for the Advancement of Colored People, which instituted many law suits to secure rights existing in the laws but in fact denied many citizens. In many cases, the laws are on the books but need the force of a lawsuit or judicial process to effectuate them.

Sometimes existing laws are activated by exerting economic pressure. For example, most states receive federal funds for worthy projects. By withholding federal funds from those states whose public officials have withheld benefits or equal treatment from certain races, the states are persuaded that it is to their best interests to comply with the laws against discrimination. This type of pressure has also been applied to public contractors who will be denied lucrative public works contracts unless they abide by laws relating to discrimination. In recent years, recourse has been had to criminal sanctions existing under legislation enacted during the reconstruction period after the Civil War.

Many civil rights laws have been passed during the past 15 years by the federal government. We can do little more than list the major legislation, in the space available in this work.

The Civil Rights Act of 1957 protected voting rights and authorized the Attorney General of the United States to institute suit when a person had been deprived of them and set up a Civil Rights Division in the Department of Justice.

The Civil Rights Act of 1960 reenforced the earlier act and contained criminal penalties for bombing and other obstruction of federal court orders.

The Civil Rights Act of 1964 prohibited discrimination in public places and in programs receiving federal funds and created an Equal Employment Opportunities Commission. It also strengthened enforcement of voting and desegregation laws.

The Voting Act of 1965 authorized the Attorney General of the United States to appoint federal examiners to register voters in areas of flagrant discrimination and increased penalties for denial of voting rights.

The Civil Rights Act of 1968 prohibited discrimination in the rental or sale of real property and protected persons pursuing specified rights -- such as attending school or employment.

Many states have taken independent action to insure civil rights to persons within their limits. There is no question but that progress is slow. Civil rights are those rights of the people to equal protection under the law, without regard to color, creed, sex, race, income. They include equality of opportunity in housing, education, employment, suffrage, public accomodations and all aspects of the judicial system. They encompass almost all of man's activities and affect every aspect of his life. As stated above, the content of these concepts included in civil rights are flexible and change with the mores of the times. Today, the term "civil rights" comes closer to meaning "human rights" and is more and more being related to the idea that there are certain attributes that attach to the state of being human, that there is a fundamental dignity in man that must not be impaired or affronted by sectarian, regional or other arbitrary action. The translation of these concepts into effective legal action is necessarily slow because, unfortunately, each man is the victim of his prejudices, and prejudices cannot be legislated away at one fell swoop but must be painstakingly eradicated, either by re-education or stern law enforcement. The rate of progress has however seen some acceleration over the past decade and a half and there is reason to believe that new generations coming up will reject "man's inhumanity to man" as inconsistent with the new life style.

Chart 1 (continued)

State	Minimum Ages F	M	Parental Consent Required if Below Age of: F	M	Medical Required for License	Waiting Period Before License	Waiting Period After License
Ohio	16	18	21	21	yes	yes--5 days	no
Oklahoma	15	18	18	21	yes	no	no
Oregon	15	18	18	21	yes	yes--7 days	no
Pennsylvania	16	16	21	21	yes	yes--3 days	no
Puerto Rico	16	18	21	21	yes	no	no
Rhode Island	16	18	21	21	yes	yes--5 days	no
South Carolina	14	16	18	18	no	yes--24 hours	no
South Dakota	16	18	18	21	yes	no	no
Tennessee	16	16	21	21	yes	yes--3 days	no
Texas	14	16	18	19	yes	no	no
Utah	14	16	18	21	yes	no	yes--5 days
Vermont	16	18	18	21	yes	no	no
Virginia	16	18	21	21	yes	no	no
Washington	17	17	18	18	no	yes--3 days	no
West Virginia	16	18	21	21	yes	yes--3 days	no
Wisconsin	16	18	18	21	yes	yes--5 days	no
Wyoming	16	18	21	21	yes	no	no

93

Chart 2
WAGES AND HOURS

State	Wages	Hours	Equal Pay for Women
Alabama	(p.w.c.) -- prevailing wage set by Com'r for each craft subject to maximum	8 h.d.; 40 h.wk. 6 d.w. for (c)	yes
Alaska	(p.w.c.) -- not less than 50¢ over prevailing federal minimum ($1.60)	(p.w.c.) -- 8 h.d. (c) -- 8 h.d.; 40 h.wk. 6 d.wk.	yes
Arizona	(p.w.c.) -- prevailing wages; for (w) & (c) min. set by Com'r	(p.w.c.) -- 8 h.d. (c) -- 8 h.d. (w) -- 8 h.d.; 48 h.wk.	yes
Arkansas	(p.w.c.) -- prevailing wages minimum -- $1.20 p.h.	(w) -- 9 h.d. (c--under 18) -- 6 d.w.; 10 h.d.; 54 h.wk. (c--under 16) -- 48 h.wk. 8 h.d.; 6 d.wk.	yes

p.w.c. -- public works contracts
w -- women
c -- children
min. -- minimum set by statute

h -- hours
d -- daily
wk -- weekly
Com'r -- Commissioner or other department head

94

Chart 2 (continued)

State	Wages	Hours	Equal Pay for Women
California	(p.w.c.) -- prevailing wages; (w) & (c) -- $1.65 exceptions not less than $1.35 p.h.	(w) -- 5 d.w.; 8 h.d., 40 h.d.; (c) -- 8 h.d., 48 h.wk.	--
Colorado	(p.w.c.) -- prevailing; Minimum -- $1.00-$1.10	(w) & (c) -- 8 h.d.; 40 h.wk.	yes
Connecticut	Min. $1.60, except as may be established by Com'r	(w) & (c) in manufacturing -- 9 h.d., 48 h.wk.; 8 h.d.; in mercantile -- 10 h.d., 6 d.wk., 48 h.wk	yes
Delaware	(p.w.c.) -- prevailing; min. -- $1.60	(c) -- 8 h.d.; 48 h.wk. (w) -- repealed	yes
District of Columbia	(p.w.c.) -- federal practice pre- vails; Minimum -- $1.60	(w) -- 8 h.d.; 6 d.wk; 48 h.wk.; (c) -- 8 h.d., 6 d.wk., 48 h.wk.	yes
Florida	(p.w.c.) -- prevailing as set by Com'r	(c) under 16 -- 40 h.wk., 8 h.d.	yes

95

Chart 2 (continued)

State	Wages	Hours	Equal Pay for Women
Georgia	Min. -- $1.25	(c) -- under 16, 8 h.d. 40 h.wk.	yes
Hawaii	(p.w.c.) -- prevailing; Min. -- $1.60	40 h.wk. (c) under 16, 8 h.d.; 40 h.wk., 6 d.wk.	yes
Idaho	Min. -- $1.25 p.h.	8 h.d., 48 h.wk. (c) under 16 -- 9 h.d.; 54 h.wk.	yes
Illinois	(p.w.c.) -- prevailing (w) & (c) -- as set by Com'r	(w) -- 8 h.d.; 48 h.wk (c) -- 6 d.wk.; 48 h.wk.	yes
Indiana	(p.w.c.) -- prevailing	(w) -- repealed (c) 14-18, 8 h.d., 40 h.wk., 6 d.wk.	yes
Iowa	- - - - -	(c) - under 16 - 8 h.d., 40 h.wk., 6 d.wk.	yes

EPILOGUE

Although no less a man than President Kennedy has said, "Ask not what your country can do for you; ask rather what you can do for your country" the truth of the matter is that the purpose of democracy or any representative form of government is to serve those who created it and whom it represents. Government is organized society. People organize to increase effectiveness of action, and to render possible activities which could not have been accomplished without a complex and sophisticated government with the great financial resources available to it. The need and desire for organization continue only as long as the government formed continues to be responsive to the needs and desires of its people.

There is today a feeling that government has failed or, at least, is failing its members; that laws do not effectively respond to the needs of the people; that laws do not protect against evils -- such as poverty, such as the deterioration of the environment, the abuses of large corporations and monied institutions. There is a feeling that the state has become a self-willed entity which is either indifferent to its members or whose aims differ from those of its members and which has developed a power of its own to thwart the will of a majority of its members.

This feeling may in part be explained by the fact that a gap always exists between the time when a change occurs in the thinking of the majority of the people and the time it is translated into effective action. Social opinions are always in advance of the law and while the gap may close, for a moment, it inevitably opens again and always tends to re-open. This is another way of saying that the law is stable -- and stability is much to be desired, for no action is predictable without this stability -- and progressive societies are in a constant state of flux. But it is nevertheless true that the happiness and welfare of a people depend greatly on the promptness with which the law responds to social needs and changed circumstances of society.

Many voices are clamoring to be heard today in America. Many serious problems exist for which solutions are sorely needed. It is perhaps paradoxical that society is in many ways calling on the law -- or the state -- to change the existing scheme of things which the state has either created or at least tolerated. But it is this very ability of a democracy to change that makes it a viable form of government. It is in this ability that the power of a representative form of government rests.

Chart 1
LEGAL AGE FOR MARRIAGE

State	Minimum Ages F	M	Parental Consent Required if Below Age of: F	M	Medical Required for License	Waiting Period Before License	Waiting Period After License
Alabama	14	17	18	21	yes	no	no
Alaska	18	19	18	19	yes	yes--3 days	no
Arizona	16	18	18	21	yes	no	no
Arkansas	16	18	18	21	yes	yes--3 days	no
California	16	18	18	21	yes	no	no
Colorado	16	16	18	21	yes	no	no
Connecticut	16	16	21	21	yes	yes--5 days	no
Delaware	16	18	18	21	yes	no	yes*
District of Columbia	16	18	18	21	yes	yes--3 days	no
Florida	16	18	21	21	yes	yes--3 days	no
Georgia	16	16	19	19	yes	yes--3 days	3 days if under age
Hawaii	16	18	15	17	yes	no	no
Idaho	18	21	16	21	yes	no	no
Illinois	16	18	18	21	yes	no	no
Indiana	16	18	18	21	yes	yes--3 days	no
Iowa	16	18	18	21	yes	yes--3 days	no

*24 hours for residents; 96 hours for out-of-state residents

Chart 1 (continued)

State	Minimum Ages F	M	Parental Consent Required if Below Age of: F	M	Medical Required for License	Waiting Period Before License	Waiting Period After License
Kansas	18	18	18	21	yes	yes--3 days	no
Kentucky	16	18	18	18	yes	yes--3 days	no
Louisiana	16	18	21	21	yes	no	yes--72 hours
Maine	16	16	18	20	yes	yes--5 days	no
Maryland	16	18	18	21	no	yes--48 hours	no
Massachusetts	12	14	16	18	yes	yes--3 days	no
Michigan	16	18	18	18	yes	yes--3 days	no
Minnesota	16	18	18	21	no	yes--5 days	no
Mississippi	15	17	18	21	no	yes--5 days	no
Missouri	15	15	18	21	yes	yes--3 days	no
Montana	16	18	18	21	yes	yes--5 days	no
Nebraska	16	18	21	21	yes	no	no
Nevada	16	18	18	21	yes	no	no
New Hampshire	13	14	18	21	yes	yes--5 days	no
New Jersey	16	18	18	21	yes	yes--72 hours	no
New York	14	16	18	21	yes	no	yes--24 hours
North Carolina	16	16	18	18	yes	no	no
North Dakota	15	18	18	21	yes	no	no

Chart 1 (continued)

State	Minimum Ages F	Minimum Ages M	Parental Consent Required if Below Age of: F	Parental Consent Required if Below Age of: M	Medical Required for License	Waiting Period Before License	Waiting Period After License
Ohio	16	18	21	21	yes	yes--5 days	no
Oklahoma	15	18	18	21	yes	no	no
Oregon	15	18	18	21	yes	yes--7 days	no
Pennsylvania	16	16	21	21	yes	yes--3 days	no
Puerto Rico	16	18	21	21	yes	no	no
Rhode Island	16	18	21	21	yes	yes--5 days	no
South Carolina	14	16	18	18	no	yes--24 hours	no
South Dakota	16	18	18	21	yes	no	no
Tennessee	16	16	21	21	yes	yes--3 days	no
Texas	14	16	18	19	yes	no	yes--5 days
Utah	14	16	18	21	yes	no	no
Vermont	16	18	18	21	yes	no	no
Virginia	16	18	21	21	yes	no	no
Washington	17	17	18	18	no	yes--3 days	no
West Virginia	16	18	21	21	yes	yes--3 days	no
Wisconsin	16	18	18	21	yes	yes--5 days	no
Wyoming	16	18	21	21	yes	no	no

Chart 2
WAGES AND HOURS

State	Wages	Hours	Equal Pay for Women
Alabama	(p.w.c.) -- prevailing wage set by Com'r for each craft subject to maximum	8 h.d.; 40 h.wk. 6 d.w. for (c)	yes
Alaska	(p.w.c.) -- not less than 50¢ over prevailing federal minimum ($1.60)	(p.w.c.) -- 8 h.d. (c) -- 8 h.d.; 40 h.wk. 6 d.wk.	yes
Arizona	(p.w.c.) -- prevailing wages; for (w) & (c) min. set by Com'r	(p.w.c.) -- 8 h.d. (c) -- 8 h.d. (w) -- 8 h.d.; 48 h.wk.	yes
Arkansas	(p.w.c.) -- prevailing wages minimum -- $1.20 p.h.	(w) -- 9 h.d. (c--under 18) -- 6 d.w.; 10 h.d.; 54 h.wk. (c--under 16) -- 48 h.wk. 8 h.d.; 6 d.wk.	yes

p.w.c. -- public works contracts
w -- women
c -- children
min. -- minimum set by statute

h -- hours
d -- daily
wk -- weekly
Com'r -- Commissioner or other department head

94

Chart 2 (continued)

State	Wages	Hours	Equal Pay for Women
California	(p.w.c.) -- prevailing wages; (w) & (c) -- $1.65 exceptions not less than $1.35 p.h.	(w) -- 5 d.w.; 8 h.d., 40 h.d.; (c) -- 8 h.d., 48 h.wk.	--
Colorado	(p.w.c.) -- prevailing; Minimum -- $1.00-$1.10	(w) & (c) -- 8 h.d.; 40 h.wk.	yes
Connecticut	Min. $1.60, except as may be established by Com'r	(w) & (c) in manufacturing -- 9 h.d., 48 h.wk.; 8 h.d.; in mercantile -- 10 h.d., 6 d.wk., 48 h.wk	yes
Delaware	(p.w.c.) -- prevailing; min. -- $1.60	(c) -- 8 h.d.; 48 h.wk. (w) -- repealed	yes
District of Columbia	(p.w.c.) -- federal practice prevails; Minimum -- $1.60	(w) -- 8 h.d.; 6 d.wk; 48 h.wk.; (c) -- 8 h.d., 6 d.wk., 48 h.wk.	yes
Florida	(p.w.c.) -- prevailing as set by Com'r	(c) under 16 -- 40 h.wk., 8 h.d.	yes

Chart 2 (continued)

State	Wages	Hours	Equal Pay for Women
Georgia	Min. -- $1.25	(c) -- under 16, 8 h.d. 40 h.wk.	yes
Hawaii	(p.w.c.) -- prevailing; Min. -- $1.60	40 h.wk. (c) under 16, 8 h.d.; 40 h.wk., 6 d.wk.	yes
Idaho	Min. -- $1.25 p.h.	8 h.d., 48 h.wk. (c) under 16 -- 9 h.d.; 54 h.wk.	yes
Illinois	(p.w.c.) -- prevailing (w) & (c) --; as set by Com'r	(w) -- 8 h.d.; 48 h.wk (c) -- 6 d.wk.; 48 h.wk.	yes
Indiana	(p.w.c.) -- prevailing	(w) -- repealed (c) 14-18, 8 h.d., 40 h.wk., 6 d.wk.	yes
Iowa	- - - -	(c) - under 16 - 8 h.d., 40 h.wk., 6 d.wk.	yes

96

Chart 2 (continued)

State	Wages	Hours	Equal Pay for Women
Kansas	(p.w.c.)--current per diem rate	(w) -- # of hrs. consonant with good health; (p.w.c.) -- 8 h.d.; (c) -- 8 h.d., 48h. wk.	yes
Kentucky	(p.w.c) -- prevailing; (w) & (c) -- set by Com'r	(w) 8 h.d., 48 h. wk. 6 d. wk.; (c) -- 8 h.d., 6 d. wk.	---
Louisiana	(p.w.c.) -- prevailing	(w) -- 9 h.d., 6 d. wk.	---
Maine	(p.w.c.) -- fair min. rate; Min. -- $1.60	(c) under 16 -- 8 h.d. 48 h. wk.	yes
Maryland	(p.w.c.) -- prevailing Min. -- $1.60	(p.w.c.) -- 8 h.d. (c) -- 8 h.d., 40 h. wk. (w) -- 10 h.d., 60 h. wk.	---
Massachusetts	(p.w.c.) -- prevailing as set by Com'r; Min. -- $1.60	(p.w.c.) -- 8 h.d., 48 h. wk. 6 d. wk.; (w) & (c) -- 48 h. wk.	yes
Michigan	(p.w.c.) -- prevailing; Min. -- $1.60	(w) -- 9 h.d., 54 h. wk. (c) -- 8 h.d., 48 h. wk.; 6 d. wk.	yes

97

Chart 2 (continued)

State	Wages	Hours	Equal Pay for Women
Minnesota	(p.w.c.) -- wage scale set by municipality (w) -- living wage as set by Com'r (c) -- same	(w) -- 54 h.wk. (c) -- 48 h.wk., 8 h.d.	- - -
Mississippi	- - - - -	(w) -- 10 h.d., 60 h.wk., (c) under 16, 8 h.d., 44 h.wk.	- - -
Missouri	(p.w.c.) -- prevailing	(w) 9 h.d.; 54 h.wk. (c) under 16-- 8 h.d., 6 d.wk., 48 h.wk.	yes
Montana	(p.w.c.) -- prevailing	(w) -- repealed (c) -- 8 h.d. (p.w.c.) -- 8 h.d.	yes
New Hampshire	(p.w.c.) -- prevailing Min. -- $1.60 p.h.	(w) & (c) -- 10 h.d. 48 h.wk.	yes
New Jersey	(p.w.c.) -- prevailing; Min. -- $1.50	(w) -- 10 h.d., 54 h.wk.; (c) under 18 -- 6 d.wk., 8 h.d. , 40 h.wk., 8 h.d.	, yes

98

Chart 2 (continued)

State	Wages	Hours	Equal Pay for Women
New Mexico	(p.w.c.) -- prevailing; Min. -- $1.60	(w) -- 8 h.d.; 48 h.wk.; (c) -- 8 h.d.; 40 h.wk.	yes
New York	(p.w.c.) -- prevailing; Min. -- $1.85	(p.w.c.) -- 8 h.d., 40 h.wk. (c) -- 8 h.d., 41 h.wk.	yes
North Carolina	Min. -- $1.25	(c) -- 9 h.d.; 48 h.wk.; (w) -- 56 h.wk.	- -
North Dakota	Com'r has power to set min.	(w) -- 8 1/2 h.d.; 48 h.wk. (c) under 16 -- 8 h.d., 48 h.wk.	- -
Ohio	(p.w.c.) -- prevailing	(p.w.c.) -- 8 h.d., 48 h.wk., state employees--40 h.wk.; (w) -- 8 h.d., 48 h.wk., (c) -- 6 d.wk., 48 h.wk., 8 h.d.	yes
Oklahoma	(p.w.c.) -- prevailing; Min. -- $1.00	(w) -- 9 h.d., 54 h.wk. (c) -- 8 h.d., 48 h.wk. (p.w.c.) -- 8 h.d.	yes

Chart 2 (continued)

State	Wages	Hours	Equal Pay for Women
Oregon	(p.w.c.) -- prevailing; Min. -- $1.25	(w) 10 h.d., 48 h.wk.; (w) -- 10 h.d., 60 h.wk. (c) -- 10 h.d., 60 h.wk.	yes
Pennsylvania	(p.w.c.) -- prevailing; Min. -- $1.60	(p.w.c.) & (w) -- 10 h.d., 48 h.wk.; (c) 10 h.d., 60 h.wk.	yes
Puerto Rico	$1.60	(c) -- 8 h.d., 48 h.wk., 208 per month; (w) 8 h.d., 48 h.wk.	yes
Rhode Island	(p.w.c.) -- prevailing	(p.w.c.) -- 8 h.d., 40 h.wk. (w) -- 9 h.d., 48 h.wk. (c) -- under 16, 8 h.d., 40 h.wk.	- -
South Carolina	$1.00	(w) -- 60 h.wk., 12 h.d.	- -
South Dakota	$1.00	(c) & (w) -- 10 h.d., 54 h.wk. (p.w.c.) -- 8 h.d., 40 h.wk., 6 d.wk.	yes

Chart 2 (continued)

State	Wages	Hours	Equal Pay for Women
Tennessee	(p.w.c.) -- prevailing	(w) -- 9 h.d., 54 h.wk.; (c) -- 8 h.d., 40 h.wk., 60 d.wk.	- -
Texas	(p.w.c.) -- prevailing Min. -- $1.40	(w) -- 9 h.d., 54 h.wk. (c) under 15 -- 8 h.d., 48 h.wk.; (p.w.c.) -- 8 h.d., 48 h.wk.	yes
Utah	(p.w.c.) -- prevailing	(w) -- 8 h.d.; 48 h.wk.; (c) -- 8 h.d.; 44 h.wk. (p.w.c.) -- 8 h.d., 48 h.wk.	- -
Vermont	(p.w.c.) -- prevailing; Min. -- $1.60	(c) under 16, 8 h.d., 6 d.wk., (w) -- restrictions removed	yes
Virginia	(p.w.c.) -- prevailing	(w) 9 h.d., 48 h.wk. (c) under 18 -- 6 d.wk., 40 h.wk.; 8 h.d.	- -
Washington	(p.w.c.) -- prevailing Min. -- $1.60	(p.w.c.) -- 8 h.d. (w) & (c) -- set by dept.	yes

Chart 2 (continued)

State	Wages	Hours	Equal Pay for Women
West Virginia	(p.w.c.) -- fair min. set by Com'r; Min. -- $1.00	48 h.wk. (c) -- 8 h.d.; 6 d.wk.., 40 h.wk.	yes
Wisconsin	(p.w.c.) -- prevailing; (w) -- $1.45 (c) under 17 -- $1.10	(p.w.c.) -- prevailing (w) -- 9 h.d., 50 h.wk.	yes
Wyoming	(p.w.c.) -- prevailing; Min. -- $1.30	(p.w.c.) -- 8 h.d. (w) -- 8 h.d. (c) -- 8 h.d.	yes

NOTES:

(1) The prevailing wage may be set by the commissioner, director of labor, or other public official; may be determined by fiscal authority of the city or locality; may be negotiated between parties.

(2) Many restrictions and limitations exist as to the employment of children including the number of hours a child may work during school year; the type of employment children of different ages may be engaged in. Similar restrictions exist in a number of states as to women employees.

Chart 3
STATE INCOME TAXES

State	Taxes	Exemptions
Alabama	first $1,000 (1.5); $1,001 - $3,000 (3); $3001-$5,000 (4.5); over $5,000 (5)	S - $1,500 M - $3,000 D - $ 300
Alaska	16% of federal tax	S - $ 625 M - $1,250 D - $ 625
Arizona	First $1,000 (2); $1,001 - $2,000 (d); $2,001 - $3,000 (4); $3,001-$4,000 (5); $4,001- $5,000 (6); $5,001-$6,000 (7); over $6,000 (8)	S - $1,000 M - $2,000 D - $ 600
Arkansas	First $3,000 (1); $3,001 - $6,000 (2); $6,001-$11,000 (3); $11,001-$25,000 (4); over $25 $25,000 (5)	S - $1,750 M - $3,250 D - $ 333
California	First $2,000 (1); $2,001 - $3,500 (2); $3,501-$5,000 (3); $5,001-$6,500 (4); $6,501- $8,000 (5); $8,001-$9,500 (6); $9,501-$11,000 (7); $11,001- $12,500 (8); $12,501-$14,000 (9); over $14,000 (10)	S - $2,250 M - $4,500 D - $ 400
Colorado	First $1,000 (1.5); $1,001 - $2,000 (2); $2,001-$3,000 (3); $3,001-$4,000 (4); $4,001- $5,000 (5); $5,001-$6,000 (5.5); $6,001-$7,000 (6); $7,001- $8,000 (6.5); $8,001-$9,000 (7); $9,001-$10,000 (7.5); over $10,000 (8)	S - $ 750 M - $1,500 D - $ 750

S - Single   M - Married or head of household   D - Dependents
(figure in parenthesis is per cent rate)

Chart 3 (continued)

State	Taxes	Exemptions
Delaware	First $1,000 (1.5); $1,001 - $2,000 (2); $2,001-$3,000 (3); $3,001-$4,000 (4); $4,001 - $5,000 (5); $5,001-$6,000 (6); $6,001-$8,000 (7); $8,001 - $30,000 (8); $30,001-$50,000 (9); $50,001-$100,000 (10); over $100,000 (11)	S - $ 600 M - $1,200 D - $ 600
Georgia	First $1,000 (1); $1,001- $3,000 (2); $3,001-$5,000 (3); $5,001-$7,000 (4); $7,001- $10,000 (5); over $10,000 (6)	S - $1,500 M - $3,000 D - $ 600
Hawaii	First $500 (2.25); $501-$1,000 (3.25); $1,001-$1,500 (4.5); $1,501-$2,000 (5); $2,001- $3,000 (6.5); $3,001-$5,000 (7.5); $5,001-$10,000 (8.5); $10,001-$14,000 (9.5); $14,001- $20,000 (10); $20,001-$30,000 (10.5); over $30,000 (11)	S - $ 625 M - $1,250 D - $ 625
Idaho	First $1,000 (3.5); $1,001- $2,000 (5); $2,001-$3,000 (6); $3,001-$4,000 (7); $4,001- $5,000 (8); over $5,000 (9)	S - $ 625 M - $1,250 D - $ 625
Illinois	Net taxable income (2.5)	S - $1,000 M - $2,000 D - $1,000
Indiana	2% of adjusted gross income	S - $1,000 M - $1,000- $2,000* D - $ 500

(*) based on adjusted gross

Chart 3 (continued)

State	Taxes	Exemptions
Iowa	First $1,000 (.75); $1,001-$2,000 (1.5); $2,001-$3,000 (2.25); $3,001-$4,000 (3); $4,001-$7,000 (3.75); $7,001-$9,000 (4.5); over $9,000 (5.25)	S - $1,500 M - $2,333 D - $ 467
Kansas	First $2,000 (2); $2,001-$3,000 (3.5) $3,001-$5,000 (4); $5,001-$7,000 (5); over $7,000 (6.25)	S - $ 625 M - $1,200 D - $ 625
Kentucky	First $3,000 (2); $3,001-$4,000 (3); $,001-$5,000 (4); $5,001-$8,000 (5); over $8,000 (6)	S - $1,000 M - $2,000 D - $1,100
Louisiana	First $10,000 (2); $10,001-$50,000 (4); over $50,000 (6)	S - $2,500 M - $5,000 D - $ 400
Maine	First $2,000 (1); $2,001-$5,000 (2); $5,001-$10,000 (3); $10,001-$25,000 (4); $25,001-$50,000 (5); over $50,000 (6)	S - $1,000 M - $2,000 D - $1,000
Maryland	First $1,000 (2); $1,001-$2,000 (3); $2,001-$3,000 (4); over $3,000 (5)	S - $ 800 M - $1,600 D - $ 800
Massachusetts	Business and earned income (4); investment income (8); annuities (2)	S - $2,000 M - $2,600-$4,000 D - $ 625
Michigan	All taxable income (2.6)	S - $1,200 M - $2,400 D - $1,200

Chart 3 (continued)

State	Taxes	Exemptions
Minnesota	First $500 (1.5); $501-$1,000 (2) $1,001-$2,000 (3); $2,001-$3,000 (5); $3,001-$4,000 (5); $4,001-$5,000 (7); $5,001-$7,000 (8); $7,001-$9,000 (9); $9,001-$12,500 (10); $12,501-$20,000 (11); over $20,000 (12)	S - $1,050 M - $1,683 D - $ 541
Mississippi	First $5,000 (2); over $5,000 (4)	S - $4,000 M - $6,000 D - ----
Missouri	First $1,000 (1); $1,001-$2,000 (1.5 less $5); $2,001-$3,000 (2 less $15); $3,001-$5,000 (2.5 less $30); $5,001-$7,000 (3 less $55); $7,001-$9,000 (3.5 less $90); over $9,000 (4 less $135); rates apply to total income	S - $ 625 M - $1,250 D - $ 625
Montana	First $1,000 (2); $1,001-$2,000 (3); $3,001-$4,000 (4); $4,001-$6,000 (4); $6,001-$8,000 (6); $8,001-$10,000 (7); $10,001-$14,000 (8); $14,001-$20,000 (9); $20,001-$35,000 (10); over $35,000 (11)	S - $ 625 M - $1,250 D - $ 625
New Hampshire	On income and dividends except interest on savings deposits (4.25)	S - $ 600 M - $1,200 D - $ ----
New Jersey	First $1,000 (2); $2,001-$3,000 (3); $3,001-$5,000 (4); $5,001-$7,000 (5); $7,001-$9,000 (6); $9,001-$11,000 (7); $11,001-$13,000 (8); $13,001-$15,000 (9);	S - $ 600 M - $1,200 D - $ 600

Chart 3 (continued)

State	Taxes	Exemptions
New Jersey (continued)	$15,001-$17,000 (10); $17,001-$19,000 (11); $19,001-$21,000 (12); $21,001-$23,000 (13); over $23,000 (14)	
New Mexico	First $10,000 (1); $10,001-$20,000 (2); $20,001-$100,000 (3); over $100,000 (4)	S - $1,500 M - $2,500 D - $ 200
New York	First $1,000 (2); $1,001-$3,000 (3); $3,001-$5,000 (4); $5,001-$7,000 (5); $7,001-$9,000 (6); $9,001-$11,000 (7); $11,001-$13,000 (8); $13,001-$15,000 (9); $15,001-$17,000 (10); $17,001-$19,000 (11); $19,001-$21,000 (12); $21,001-$23,000 (13); over $23,000 (14)	S - $ 625 M - $1,250 D - $ 625
	(Tax credits of $12.50 to singles and married persons filing separate returns; $25 tax credit for head of household and married persons filing joint returns.)	
North Carolina	First $2,000 (3); $2,001-$4,000 (4); $4,001-$6,000 (5); $6,001-$10,000 (6); over $10,000 (7)	S - $1,000 M - $2,000 D - $ 300
North Dakota	First $3,000 (1); $3,001-$4,000 (2); $4,001-$5,000 (3); $5,001-$6,000 (5); $6,001-$8,000 (7.5); $8,001-$15,000 (10); over $15,000 (11)	S - $ 600 M - $1,500 D - $ 600

107

Chart 3 (continued)

State	Taxes	Exemptions
Oklahoma	First $1,500 (1); $1,501-$3,000 (2); $3,001-$4,500 (3); $4,501-$6,000 (4); $6,001-$7,500 (5); over $7,500 (6)	S - $1,000 M- $2,000 D- $ 500
Oregon	First $500 (4); $501-$1,000 (5); $1,001-$1,500 (6); $1,501-$2,000 (7); $2,001-$3,000 (8); $3,001-$4,000 (9); $4,001-$8,000 (10.2); over $8,000 (11.6)	S- $ 600 M- $ 1,200 D- $ 600
South Carolina	First $2,000 (2); $2,001-$4,000 (3); $4,001-$6,000 (4); over $6,000 (5)	S- $ 600 M- $ 1,200
Tennessee	Interest and dividends (6% but dividends from corporations having 75% of its property in Tennessee, ad valorem tax of 4%)	S ------- ------- -------
Utah	First $1,000 (2); $1,001-$2,000 (2); $2,001-$3,000 (3); $3,001-$4,000 (4); over $4,000 (5)	S- $ 600 M- $ 1,200 D- $ 600
Vermont	First $1,000 (2) $1,001-$3,000 (4); $3,001-$5,000 (6); over $5,000 (7.5). Note: subject to reduction if surplus in general funds permit.	S- $ 500 M- $1,000 D- $ 500
Virginia	First $3,000 (2); $3,001-$5,000 (3); over $5,000 (5)	S- $1,000 M-$2,000 D-$ 200

Chart 3 (continued)

State	Taxes	Exemptions
West Virginia	First $2,000 (2.1); $2,001-$4,000 (2.3); $4,001-$6,000 (2.8); $6,001-$8,000 (3.2); $8,001-$10,000 (3.5); $10,001-$12,000 (4.0); $12,001- $14,000 (4.6); $14,001-$16,000 (4.9); $16,001 -$18,000 (5.3); $18,001-$2,000 (5.4); $2,001-$2,2000 (6.0); $22001-$2,600 (6.1); $2,6001-$32,000 (6.5); $32,001-$38,000 (6.8); $38,00;-$44,000 (7.2); $50,001-$60,000 (7.9); $60,001-$70,000 (8.2); $70,001-$80,000 (8.6); $80,00;-$90,000 (8.8); $90,001-$100,000 (9.1); $100,001-$150,000 (9.3); $150,001- $200,000 (9.5); over $200,000 (9.6)	S- $ 625 M- $1,250 D- $ 625
Wisconsin	First $1,000 (1); $1,000-$2,000 (1.25); $2,001-$3,000 (1.5); $3,001-$4,000 (2.5); $4,001-$5,000 (3); $5,001-$6,000 (3.5); $6,00;-$7,000 (4); $7,001-$8,000 (5); each additional $1,000 is taxed at rate 1/4 of 1% more than preceding thousand until income is $14,000 (8); over $14,000 (8.5); surtax of 20% in effect	S- $ 700 M- $ 1,320 D- $ 560
Wyoming	none	

109

Chart 4
STATE SALES AND USE TAXES

2% sales and use tax
Indiana   Oklahoma

2-1/2 % sales and use tax
Nebraska

3% sales and use tax

Arizona	Iowa	Missouri	Vermont
Arkansas	Kansas	Nevada	Virginia
Colorado	Louisiana	New York	West Virginia
Georgia	Massachusetts	North Carolina	Wyoming
Idaho	Minnesota	Tennessee	

3-1/4% sales and use tax
Texas

4% sales and use tax

Alabama	Florida	Michigan	South Carolina
California	Hawaii	New Mexico	South Dakota
District of	Illinois	North Dakota	Utah
Columbia	Maryland	Ohio	Wisconsin

4-1/2% sales and use tax
Washington

5% sales and use tax

Connecticut(*)	Mississippi
Kentucky	New Jersey
Maine	Rhode Island

6% sales and use tax
Pennsylvania

The above taxes are those set by the state. Additional sales taxes are levied by the cities, under enabling legislation passed by the states.

(*) The Connecticut state sales and use tax will be 3-1/2% starting July 1, 1971.

The above taxes are applicable to retail sale of personal property.

GLOSSARY

ABANDONMENT OF CHILD -- Desertion of a child with the intention to forego parental duties and responsibilities

ABANDONMENT OF SPOUSE -- The act of a husband or wife who leaves his or her spouse willfully with the intention of causing a permanent separation

ABORTION -- The expulsion of the fetus (the unborn child) at a time when it has not acquired the power of sustaining an independent life

ADDICTION -- Habitual, uncontrollable use of narcotics

ADMINISTRATOR, ADMINISTRATRIX--A person, or corporation, appointed by the court to represent the estate of a deceased person who died without a will, to manage the estate and distribute the property

ADOPTION -- Formal procedure by means of which a parent-child relationship is created between persons not so related by blood

ADULTERY -- Sexual intercourse between persons, one of whom is married to another

AGE OF CONSENT -- Age fixed by statute to denote the time of life at which a person may marry without parental consent

ALIMONY -- An allowance set by the court for the support and maintenance of a spouse, or divorced spouse, in lieu of marital support; alimony is separate and different from support due the children of the marriage

ANATOMICAL GIFT -- A gift of bodily organ or tissues or any part of the body

ANNUITIES -- Yearly, or periodic, payments of money for a definite period of time or for the life of the person entitled to receive the same

ANNULMENT OF MARRIAGE -- The judicial determination that a marriage is a nullity for reasons existing at the time the marriage was solemnized

ARTIFICIAL INSEMINATION -- Means of impregnating a woman other than by sexual intercourse

ASSIGNED RISK POOL -- This is a "pool" of insurance companies who supply automobile insurance where the insured is not insurable by an insurance company of his own choice

BANKRUPT -- A person who is incapable of meeting his debts, an insolvent; in a stricter legal sense, he is a person who has committed acts prejudicial to his creditors, or one who is qualified under the bankruptcy laws, to file a voluntary petition to be declared a bankrupt

BENEFICIARY -- One receiving benefits, profits or advantages; the beneficiary of life insurance policy is the person entitled to receive the proceeds thereof

BEQUEST -- A gift of personal property by will; a legacy

BONA FIDE RESIDENCE -- A residence which is intended as the domicile of the person

CAPITAL GAINS AND LOSSES -- gains or losses resulting from the sale or exchange of capital goods; that is, other than income or interest

CAVEAT EMPTOR -- Let the buyer beware -- in other words, the buyer must examine, judge and test for himself the product involved

CHARGE ACCOUNT -- A mortgage on personal property -- a transfer of a right in personal property to insure payment of an obligation of the person who executes the mortgage

CHILD ABUSE -- Mistreatment of children, generally by a parent or other relative or person encharged with the custody of the children, which is sufficient to warrant the removal of the children from the custody of such parent or guardian

CITATION -- A notice issuing from a court advising the person to whom it is directed that certain proceedings will take place at a stated time and place

CIVIL RIGHTS -- Rights which belong to every citizen or resident of a state or country, including the rights of property, marriage, protection by the laws, freedom of contract, trial by jury and many others; rights insured to a person in his individual capacity by the Constitution of the United States and of the states

CLOSING -- A term used to describe the transaction involving the signing of a contract for the purchase of real property (contract closing) or the transfer of title to real property (title closing) at which time, matters open between the parties are adjusted

CODICIL -- A codification of the terms of a will, in writing, which forms part of the will; it is executed with all the formality and in compliance with all the technicalities of a will

CO-INSURANCE -- When a person is under-insured, he bears part of a loss; to this extent, he is a co-insurer

COLLECTIVE BARGAINING -- Dealings between employer and employees, the latter acting through designated employee representatives

COMMON LAW MARRIAGE -- Marriage not solemnized in compliance with the formal requirements of the state, followed by open co-habitation between the parties who hold themselves out to be married to each other

COMMUNITY PROPERTY -- Property owned jointly by a husband and wife, property acquired by either spouse during the marriage, when not acquired as the separate property of either

COMPETENT PERSON -- As opposed to an incompetent person, is one who possesses the natural or legal qualifications of a legally capable person

CONDOMINIUM -- Literally, joint ownership of property; in modern usage, it refers to a unit in a multi-unit dwelling, owned by one person who also owns, in common with other tenants, all the other parts of the building used in common (such as stairways, lobbies, corridors, etc.)

CONSUMERISM -- The philosophy of the protection of consumer

CONTRIBUTION -- An insurance term; in fire insurance, if there are several policies covering the same risk, the loss is prorated among the insurers

COOPERATIVES -- Refers to ownership of property; in a cooperative, each resident has an interest in the real property, usually represented by shares of stock of the corporation, and the right to occupy one dwelling unit within the building

CREDIT -- The financial reputation of a person, on the basis of which he may borrow money or obtain goods on time

CURTESY -- The right of a married man to a life estate in real property of his deceased wife, if there has been issue of the marriage; this right has been abolished in many states

DECREE -- A determination of the rights of the parties in certain proceedings

DEVISE -- A gift of real property by will

DISCRIMINATION -- A breach of duty to treat all persons alike; discrimination may be because of color, creed, race, sex or on other grounds

DISSOLUTION OF MARRIAGE -- Termination of marriage, generally because of fraudulent representations of one party to the other

DISTRIBUTEE -- A person entitled to share in the estate of a person dying without a will

DIVORCE -- Legal termination of a marriage

DOMICILE --The legal residence of a person

DOUBLE JEOPARDY -- The principle that a person shall not be brought into danger of punishment (or trial) for the same offense more than once

DOWER -- A wife's right to share in the real estate owned by her husband at time of his death; abolished in most American jurisdictions

ECOLOGY -- The science of man's environment

ELECTION, RIGHT OF -- The right of a surviving spouse to share in the estate of a deceased person by electing against a will where the provisions of the will are less favorable

EMINENT DOMAIN -- The right of the state to take real property belonging to private persons for public use, usually compensating the latter for such taking

ENDOWMENT -- A fund payable under an insurance policy to a named person at a certain time, or at his death

ENTIRETY -- Joint ownership between a husband and wife, unless otherwise specifically defined

ESCHEAT -- Return of property of a person who died without person who could inherit from him to the state of his domicile

EXECUTOR (EXECUTRIX) -- A person or corporation named in a will to carry out the provisions of it and to make distribution under it

EX PARTE DIVORCE -- Is a divorce obtained without the appearance in court or by pleading of one spouse

GUARANTY -- A collateral agreement for the payment of another's debt if the latter fails to pay it

HEIRS AT LAW -- Those designated by law to succeed to the property of a deceased person

HOLOGRAPHIC WILL -- One written entirely in the hand of the testator and signed by him

ILLEGITIMATE -- A person born out of lawful wedlock

INHERITANCE -- Property descending to an heir

INTESTATE -- A person dying without a will

LEGACY -- A disposition of property by will

LETTERS OF ADMINISTRATION -- Documents issued by the appropriate court to the administrator of an estate to vest him with authority to handle the estate of a person who died without a will

LETTERS TESTAMENTARY -- Document of authority issued by appropriate court to executor of estate of a person who died leaving a will

MAJORITY -- As used in this work, the age at which a person may act independently of a parent or guardian, usually age 21 years

MINIMUM WAGES -- The amount designated by statute as the least amount payable as wages; may be effective only as to certain trades industries or general in application

MISCEGENATION -- Marriage or intercourse between persons of different races; this has been held to be criminal in some states

NECESSARIES -- In reference to a wife and children, those things which are suited to a wife or child's station in life, their needs and wants, within the economic limits of the husband required to supply them

NEXT OF KIN -- Persons entitled to share in personal property of a decedent who dies without a will

NON-CUPATIVE WILL -- An unwritten will, made by a soldier, sailor, in active military duty or a mariner at sea, in immediate peril of death

OMBUDSMAN -- A civilian watch dog; a person or group engaged in the protection of the public, against public officials and others. The idea originated in Sweden over 150 years ago where it was directed primarily against public officials. Today, it has spread so that even corporations have their own ombudsmen to protect consumers against corporate action

PLEDGE -- The turning over of personal property as security for a debt or obligation, with the right to sell upon the failure of the debtor to meet the obligation

PREVAILING WAGES-- Those wages which have been determined to be in general effect in the trade or occupation under consideration

PRIMOGENITURE -- A rule of inheritance by means of which the first son inherits all his father's estate, if he survives the father; this rule is now obsolete

PRIVILEGED COMMUNICATION -- A communication between persons in a confidential relationship which, because of this relationship, may not be disclosed to others without the consent of the person who made it. This privilege exists as to statements made by one spouse to the other; between attorney and client, doctor and patient; confessor and penitent

PROBATE (of will) -- A court proceeding by means of which the validity of a will is "proved" and the will is ordered entered in the records of the court and becomes effective

PUBLIC ADMINISTRATOR -- A public official designated by the court to administer the estate of a deceased person where there is no competent person related by blood or marriage to the deceased person to serve as administrator

RECIDIVISM -- Habitual return to crime; a relapse into crime after having once been convicted

REHABILITATION -- The restoration of a sick criminal or disabled person; or the restoration of an addict to useful life and abstinence from drugs

RIPARIAN RIGHTS -- Rights in water existing as natural and inherent incidents of ownership of land through which or along which that water runs

SECURED DEBT -- An obligation secured by a mortgage or other right against property of the debtor

SELF-INCRIMINATION, Right against -- Right not to speak if by speaking one renders oneself liable to criminal proceedings or incrimination

SEPARATION -- A judicial separation (usually referring to one other than a divorce which terminates the marriage for all purposes). A separation decree involves the physical separation of spouses

SEPARATION AGREEMENT -- An agreement between husband and wife not to live together, usually containing provisions for the wife and children's support

SOCIAL SECURITY LAW -- A federal law which provides for the establishment of old age assistance, old age and survivors insurance benefits and unemployment insurance plus other benefits

SOLEMNIZATION OF MARRIAGE -- The performance of a ceremony by which a man and a woman contract a marriage

SUCCESSION -- The taking of property by inheritance -- either
by will or the laws of intestacy

SURETY -- A person who answers for the debts of another and
whose duty to pay is not conditioned on the failure of the
other to make payment

SUPPORT (of family) -- The duty of a husband arising out of the
marital status and imposed by law, to provide his wife and
family with a place to live, the necessaries and comforts
of life, suitable to the rank and condition of the husband and
wife and the means and earning power of the husband

TESTATOR (TESTATRIX) -- A person who makes a will

INDEX